Energy Vampires

How to Protect Yourself From Toxic People

(Managing Stress & Negative Thoughts in Your Personal & Professional Life)

James Zamudio

Published By **Ryan Princeton**

James Zamudio

Energy Vampires: How to Protect Yourself From Toxic People (Managing Stress & Negative Thoughts in Your Personal & Professional Life)

ISBN 978-1-9992226-2-8

No part of this guidebook shall be reproduced in any form without permission in writing from the publisher except in the case of brief quotations embodied in critical articles or reviews.

Legal & Disclaimer

The information contained in this book is not designed to replace or take the place of any form of medicine or professional medical advice. The information in this book has been provided for educational & entertainment purposes only.

The information contained in this book has been compiled from sources deemed reliable, and it is accurate to the best of the Author's knowledge; however, the Author cannot guarantee its accuracy and validity and cannot be held liable for any errors or omissions. Changes are periodically made to this book. You must consult your doctor or get professional medical advice before using any of the suggested remedies, techniques, or information in this book.

Upon using the information contained in this book, you agree to hold harmless the Author from and against any damages, costs, and expenses, including any legal fees potentially resulting from the application of any of the information provided by this guide. This disclaimer applies to any damages or injury caused by the use and application, whether directly or indirectly, of any advice or information presented, whether for breach of contract, tort, negligence, personal injury, criminal intent, or under any other cause of action.

You agree to accept all risks of using the information presented inside this book. You need to consult a professional medical practitioner in order to ensure you are both able and healthy enough to participate in this program.

Table Of Contents

Chapter 1: Psychic Empath?

Are you a psychic empath or are you in reality an empathetic individual? Sometimes the line among the ones may be blurry. Even the person who struggles with empathy once in a while has days when they truly appear to enjoy excellent human beings's ache. This might be circumstantial. For instance, you are in all likelihood to feel extra empathetic inside the course of someone who is closer to you than someone you've in reality met. You may moreover expand empathy more with out problem if you've been via the equal scenario in the beyond. That being said, an empath sincerely has traits that stand out on the subject of the manner they percentage in distinct people's feelings of ache.

Unlike the commonplace empathetic character who has their off days wherein they don't appear to care about definitely every person else but themselves, psychic empaths every now and then have any downtime. They experience and experience strength right from the right away they awaken to the time they go to mattress besides they recognize the way to guard themselves.

There are some significantly distinguishing trends that set aside the psychic empath. These are elaborated within the segment beneath:

Qualities of a Psychic Empath

You are aware about the whole lot round and in you

The commonplace man or woman is often aware of what is going on in their lifestyles, at the least to an inexpensive quantity. They can inform what they're thinking about, they're peripherally aware about what is taking vicinity in their out of doors surroundings, and they will be capable of take a look at the verbal and seen cues from the humans they're surrounded by way of. A psychic empath takes this a notch better. They can sense quite a lot everything in themselves and their outside environment. They are in a function to walk in a room and right now study the mood of the room. They can inform while a person is getting irritated or disillusioned even earlier than it shows on their face. If you are a psychic empath, you may locate yourself being very privy to what is taking place for your existence or maybe inside the lives of the people you care approximately. If a chum goes through a heartbreak, you will percent their pain in a manner that others can not, even earlier than your buddy makes this pain public knowledge.

You hate crowds and prefer being on my own

While you care loads about people, you furthermore may favor to interact with them on a one-on-one foundation and not even as they are in a crowd. You discover crowds overwhelming and like to hold your very very own employer. You like solitude because it allows you to recharge your power. You can not stay to tell the tale for lengthy in a crowd setting. Crowds steal your satisfaction; they make you nervous and worrying and that they drain you. The reason why crowds drain you so with out problems is due to the fact you're constantly deciding on up power alerts from human beings and being in a crowd manner you are bombarded with such some of indicators which you get overwhelmed. Do you select out staying indoors to going out? Are you the type of man or woman who may additionally need to as an opportunity watch a stay performance on TV than certainly attend the concert in person?

You are an amazing listener

A downside of being referred to as a fantastic listener is that humans typically tend to take that as their cue to sell off all their troubles on you. If you have got got been suspecting all along that you are an empath, that is a hassle that you in all likelihood have. Empaths are frequently keen to virtually apprehend humans and that they are attempting this by way of listening greater than they talk. People love pinnacle listeners. Most human beings love speaking approximately themselves and will gravitate in the direction of absolutely everyone who offers them the chance. Because of your correct listening capabilities, you can have discovered yourself playing therapist to friends and strangers alike. Unfortunately for you, you cannot have an entire lot of empaths on your lifestyles who pass returned the choice. The magazine you write in every night time in advance than you go to mattress might be the simplest listening ear that you switch to after you've got were given spent your entire day being attentive to other humans rant approximately everything and something.

You are notably emotional and often moody

An empath feels their emotions after which feels one-of-a-kind human beings's feelings. Naturally, there can be going to be an entire lot of moodiness taking vicinity. Imagine having to address the feelings of six human beings interior an hour. How might also that make you revel in? Moody, at splendid and murderous at worst. This is the every day catch 22 situation of an empath. They may match away their residence feeling all happy and content material most effective to enjoy six one in each of a kind feelings even in advance than they get to art work. If you have someone on your lifestyles who seems to have a present day emotion every hour, it is probably that they're an empath whose emotions are linking with the emotions of different human beings. Do not choose out them unfairly.

You frequently feel emotionally and mentally tired

As a psychic empath, it is herbal to experience depleted on the give up of the day when you have used up all the emotional, intellectual, and physical assets which can be to be had to you. It may be in particular daunting in case you are working in a scenario in that you're constantly exposed to those who are in pain or who're disillusioned. What makes it worse is that there are individuals who consciously drain your strength from you after they determine out that you are an empath. These people are known as power vampires. Chapter 3 delves into the information of a way to discover an energy vampire on pinnacle of sharing a few smooth approaches that you can rent to protect yourself while faced with an energy vampire.

Kids and animals evidently gravitate toward you

Kids and pets aren't recognized to be articulate as some distance as speakme one-of-a-kind humans's intentions. However, they will be every especially intuitive. What younger kids and animals lack in conversation abilities they make up for in instinct. Intuition is described because of the fact the capability to recognize instinctively without relying on aware reasoning. What this shows is that a toddler will instinctively realize which you are an terrific man or woman with out going thru the steps of logical reasoning. The same case applies to pets. If you're the individual that the dog runs to every time in spite of the fact that there are one of a kind humans in the room, then probably you want to start searching at yourself extra in any other case. Especially if the other signs of the psychic empath as listed above already exercising to you.

You struggle with intimate relationships

As an empath; it isn't always unusual to battle with the want to be cherished at the identical time as moreover looking to be on my own. Togetherness may not be your cup of tea, specifically on the identical time as this togetherness technique being overloaded each day. Psychic empaths ought to undergo a extensive form of feelings as they have interaction with human beings daily. When they're given a choice to be in a dating or not, many psychic empaths want the possibility to be by myself actually due to the reality it is so an entire lot less complex than being with a person. It's now not that they need to be on my own all the time; it is certainly that they've gone through the motions of being emotionally tired and they virtually do not revel in like going thru it another time. It can be pretty the sensitive balancing act, and commonly you may locate yourself pushing humans away. Some humans might also moreover anticipate that you are sincerely frightened of willpower with out know-how which you are healing your self from emotional scars and do now not want to take any greater on board.

Spirituality resonates with you

There are many one-of-a-type religions within the global with all varieties of guidelines and ideologies. However, those varieties of strict tips of what you may and cannot do actually don't make experience to you. When a person who is gifted with outstanding instinct, they instinctively apprehend what is morally right and wrong and abide their non-public natural jail pointers that revel in right to them. In modern worldwide, the only concept that looks to make revel in to the empath is spirituality. Spirituality is a huge idea, giving the empath a revel in of freedom, encouraging a direction of self-discovery, increase, and connectedness.

Spirituality additionally expresses the perception that we are aside of a few factor an entire lot massive than this just this physical global. We aren't a human having a physical experience. We are in reality, an eternal soul having a human enjoy. And this resonates properly for the Empath because it ties in with their more cause of helping people in the bodily global and growing the Earth awareness.

You love connecting with nature

Granted, many humans want to appreciate the beauty of the natural international. For you, even though, the relationship feels deeper and more private. You want to thieve moments on the park, and your ideal domestic might be a cabin within the woods surrounded with the aid of manner of the factors of hobby and sounds of the wild. Nature replenishes your power. You love the greenery of wood, the ocean, and you adore to spend some time hiking within the trails. You are in no way unhappy at the same time as you're out and approximately exploring the herbal wonders of the Universe. After getting your strength sapped through those around you, you like the comfort of knowing that nature can repair this strength to the ultimate bit.

You have been accused of being too nice

Empaths in truth do have hearts of gold. The problem with that is that they do not realise at the same time as to save you pouring into others. If you're a psychic empath that allows you to offer the final blouse in your once more, you likely have some nicely friends who have picked up at the same. These are the friends who will accuse you of being too first-rate and inform you which you need to prevent giving an excessive amount of to people due to the truth they're capable of see how loads it drains you. What your friends won't understand is that your generosity is ingrained on your DNA.

You have a totally active thoughts

Most Empaths are pretty introverted, which means that they may be in their head loads. Thinking, watching, daydreaming, visualizing, reflecting and growing. Empaths view the sector completely excellent to the not unusual man or woman. This with their proficient intuition, comes a amazing factor, to create many exceptional matters to impact the arena notably.

However, that is generally restrained, in particular within the empaths early adventure from topics along with loss of self perception, low self- genuinely nicely well worth, fear, doubt and uncertainty. Over time because the empath listens to their intuition and specializes in ridding those low vibrational functions, life turns into exciting.

Struggles of an Empath

As an empath, you could likely have struggles that non-empaths cannot become privy to with. Simple situations that non-empaths can effects deal with (due to the fact they aren't the use of an entire lot in their emotional assets) will speedy drain you and leave you feeling beaten. Empaths regularly discover themselves struggling on a each day basis, and it can be even greater tough even as you do not already understand which you are an empath. As such, you could find out your self wondering why you have a tendency to react in a selected way while the humans spherical you seem to take the entirety of their stride.

Mainstream media is overwhelming and draining

While most human beings take a look at television as a shape of enjoyment and a method to unwind after an extended day, empaths often have quite the opportunity outlook. Television shows can be especially draining for an empath because of the myriad of feelings that producers and administrators are aiming to elicit out in their target market. What's extra, the statistics has grow to be in place of a horror display in itself. Whether statistics anchors are reporting about the extremely-modern-day Middle East catastrophe or looming wars among dissenting countries, it most effective takes minutes in advance than the empath begins their downward spiral into ugly feelings.

Empaths don't like pronouncing no

Empaths moreover frequently warfare with pronouncing no to others. Most people, empaths or now not, do not like to say no to others. There is a effective struggle that contains denying someone what they need, even on the same time as you recognize it's for the splendid. It is not for now not anything that there are campaigns geared closer to supporting others understand that "no" is a whole statement and answer on its very personal. When you are saying no to someone's request, there are regularly poor feelings so that you can consist of the resource of as a end result. There might be guilt or perhaps resentment. Empaths hate managing horrible feelings. They choose to say "certain" because of the reality they favor to make specific human beings happy. At the equal time, they do no longer need to cope with any awful emotions that might cease result from turning down a person's request due to the fact then they is probably drained by means of the use of those bad emotions. At the surrender of the day, empaths discover themselves in a instead hard position wherein they need to learn to create boundaries by manner of manner of saying no however additionally guard their electricity with the resource of mastering how to mention no within the maximum tactful way feasible.

Empaths struggle with crowds and group interactions

Imagine being able to select out up people's energies in truth by using manner of manner of being in their presence. How might that make you revel in? For a moment, it is probably amusing information that you may observe someone with out even trying to invite what they will be feeling. After some time despite the fact that, you will likely turn out to be overwhelmed to the difficulty wherein you'll not have any preference to recognize what someone is going through. This is the lifestyles of an empath on a each day basis. When they'll be out shopping in stores or taking part in an afternoon on the seashore, empaths can pick up all the electricity spherical them. This might be a laugh if all this changed into extraordinary electricity but sadly, in most times, it isn't always. As such, social situations that offer a laugh mingling opportunities for non-empaths come to be being pretty the possibility for them. Often, empaths will pick out to retreat to their non-public solitude. As a result, they get classified as loners or introverts whilst in reality they in fact want on the way to enjoy companionship with out getting too crushed.

Empaths are at excessive threat for addiction

What takes place at the same time as an empath gets uninterested in feeling crushed? They search for a way out. An empath who is uninterested in going through the rollercoaster of emotion and power will search for some thing to assuage themselves and quiet the chaos with. In many times, this finally ends up being a horrible addiction, that could ultimately end up an addiction. Many addicts are regularly empaths who've been going through a length of ache and wound up on the incorrect course. This isn't always to mean that every one addicts are empaths although. It is essential for the psychic empath to update the ones lousy addictions with 'awesome addictions.' For instance, mastering a way to play the guitar or taking walks out on the gymnasium.

Empaths have a difficult time keeping jobs

Another vicinity that empaths struggle with is the area of employment. Anybody who has ever had a task will outcomes will can help you understand that jobs are not usually fun. There are days while you may display up simply due to the truth you need a paycheck. For empaths, this form of tolerance for some element that isn't always thrilling is probably hard to come decrease again thru. It is specially daunting for an empath to paintings in a piece environment that is toxic. As such, many empaths conflict to maintain jobs or even once they do hold the roles, they could have a difficult time developing to the pinnacle. Most oldsters which are non-empaths can also find out it smooth to live sane in a aggressive and brutal place of work in which throwing every unique under the bus is the norm. However, an empath will battle with the feelings that come about because of this behavior. Empaths will always be in search of jobs that deliver them pride and satisfaction. Given the dominion of the present day global, there are not many roles that during form those necessities and mainly now not in the corporate realm. As a end result, you will in all likelihood discover in your lifestyles hopping from manner to interest for reasons that do not make experience to you. Why can't you maintain down a undertaking? Blame your heightened experience of empathy. Working for yourself can be a brilliant alternative for empaths.

Empaths are frequently worn-out

Do you frequently experience worn-out and fatigued? You honestly is probably managing one of the many struggles of an empath. Many empaths experience exhausted on the forestall of the day due to the severa emotions that they go through whilst interacting with others. You might discover yourself questioning how worn-out someone who sits at a desk all day could possibly probable be. Truth is, the place of job empath will spend eight hours absorbing and managing the power of thier colleagues, only to find out themselves actually fatigued on the stop of the day. When he/she goes domestic, this empath might probable discover themselves in a space wherein they maintain to take in the energy of the humans they percent a domestic with. If the ones human beings are not emitting actual energy, the empath will keep to get tired. This will maintain at the equal time as they sleep (assuming they share a bed with someone), and in the morning they may awaken without the gain of a clean night time of sleep. It is simple to peer that the empath goes via a in no manner-completing cycle of emotional and highbrow drain. It may be particularly difficult to keep a healthy stability of feeling and recuperation as an empath. If you are constantly taking over the feelings of others with out prioritizing your self, there may be a high risk that you could burn yourself out.

Many human beings like to take advantage of empaths

Even after they do not advocate to region themselves in that lure 22 state of affairs, empaths frequently discover themselves because the delegated dumping floor for all varieties of emotional rubbish. Friends, family, colleagues or even strangers regularly use empaths as their structures for unloading every emotional and intellectual baggage that they will have. Since empaths no longer often say no (and are such unique listeners), they're regularly left to mop up the mess left within the returned of, whilst the opposite birthday party movements on with the consolation of getting gotten some component off their chest.

They war to articulate who or what they may be

A lot of psychic empaths warfare with their self-identification. This is usually a result of the conflicting, and frequently demeaning, messages that they've heard approximately themselves all their lives. When a psychic empath grows up in a own family that they are not listened to or disregarded as being dramatic or too emotional, they retreat proper into a shell for safety features. In this shell, the psychic empath wonders approximately who they will be.

Am I simply honestly too emotional?

Am I being too dramatic? Am I overreacting?

Am I right in behaving in this way or will I come off as being too sensitive?

What is wrong with being too sensitive besides?

These are all questions that an empath can also war with. Such questions breed self-doubt and self-doubt is frequently the basis motive of low self-worth and identification issues, which might be all struggles that empaths generally face.

They may additionally struggle with melancholy and tension

Because of the myriad feelings that psychic empath is going via, and the fact that they not often get any help for it, there can be a excessive chance for the improvement of depression and tension. Of route, this isn't to mention that psychic empaths are all depressed and worrying. The fact of the problem; however, is that psychic empaths are mainly predisposed to despair and tension because of the truth they will be basically emotional sponges. They mop up emotional spills and preserve them in. When those spills accumulate within the empath without a healthful outlet, there can be a outstanding hazard for despair and distinct temper troubles.

They war with non-public relationships

Imagine being able to pick out up the feelings of all people spherical you. How could likely this modification your belief of relationships? You is probably unwilling to get too near human beings due to the fact you discover them an excessive amount of to address. You might be now not capable of confront the feelings which you arouse in one of a kind people, specifically while these emotions are the ones of pain, unhappiness, anger or possibly hate. In brief, you can now not do very well with getting close to people. Couple this with the truth that many empaths are introverted and stay inner their heads and you've got your self a recipe that doesn't permit for notably many non-public or intimate relationships. While the empath might also want to experience close and cherished, they prefer their downtime lots too. Striking a stability among being cherished and being left alone is virtually a few problem that many empaths struggle with.

Dealing with Narcissists

It isn't always uncommon for an empath to have experienced or handled a narcissist of their existence. In maximum times, it's far both professional via the use of a narcissistic decide or narcissistic companion or both. As we recognize, empaths have pleasant empathy. Narcissists, however, are incapable of expressing any symptoms of empathy. To the narcissist, people are considered as gadgets that may be manipulated as even though they had been on a chess board in case you want to serve the narcissists very very very own wishes. Empaths appear to find out themselves entangled regularly inside the narcissist's net of deception basically due to the fact it's so smooth for the narcissist to govern them, mainly if the empath is early in the procedure of self-discovery.

Overcoming narcissists, but, is a natural a part of the technique as we're capable of apprehend crimson flags a first rate deal higher inside the destiny and make certain extra protection. They moreover mirror our susceptible factors that we want to artwork on that allows you to grow to be a extra empowered person. An empowered empath will not be susceptible to the manipulation and mind approaches of a narcissist.

Chapter 2: Types Of Psychic Empaths

Psychic empaths are not all alike. There are unique forms of psychic empaths, relying on how they enjoy electricity spherical them. The six precise sorts of psychic empaths embody the emotional empath, the claircognizant empath, the geomantic empath, the telepathic empath, the precognitive empath, and the psychometric empath.

Emotional Empath

This is the maximum common form of psychic empath. An emotional empath is able to pick out up the feelings of the humans around them very effects. They can sense the disappointment of a unhappy individual and the pleasure of a glad man or woman as even though those emotions had been their non-public. If an emotional empath isn't always self-aware and capable to distinguish their feelings and people of others, then they are able to end up emotionally worn-out right away. If you undergo in thoughts your self an emotional empath, it is essential which you discover ways to step decrease again and address yourself so that you do not get mentally or emotionally worn-out.

Claircognizant Empath

Sometimes called an intuitive empath, the claircognizant empath is capable of observe special humans certainly by using way of being in their presence. Claircognizant empaths are difficult to misinform due to the fact they may be capable of recognize lies notwithstanding the fact that the character is making an attempt their top notch to mask their intentions. If you're capable of examine someone and right away experience the energies of deceit around them you then without a doubt is probably a claircognizant empath. If you're this form of empath, you may choose to surround yourself with people who've proper and clean power that aligns together in conjunction with your private.

Besides being capable of effortlessly check humans's intentions, you could apprehend which you have claircognizance if you seem to revel in coincidences greater than the common character. For instance, you may in all likelihood pick up your phone to name your superb buddy handiest for the cellphone to start ringing. The name at the caller ID? Your exceptional buddy. You furthermore look like brimming with new and top notch mind that you can't wait to percentage with others. Claircognizant empaths are frequently very creative and innovative. They make for terrific musicians and writers because of the fact they will experience what exclusive people want, and then articulate this flawlessly.

Geomantic Empath

A geomantic empath has the ability to have a look at and understand the energies given off via manner of the planet. In other terms, they may communicate with the surroundings round them. How do in case you are a geomantic empath? A key sign to appearance out for is even as you experience a strong connection in the direction of a place or if a selected vicinity strongly repels you. It may be because of the reality you're deciding on up energy that you each like plenty or strongly resent from a specific location. Geomantic empaths normally have a propensity to have the potential to inform at the same time as a natural disaster is oncoming. For instance, they may enjoy whilst a tsunami is on the manner even earlier than the meteorological branch problems an alarm. Many animals have a propensity to have geomantic empathy. They will, as an example, run and cowl for canopy in advance than the onset of a tsunami.

Telepathic Empath

In the remarkable phrases, a telepathic empath is a mind reader. They can inform what is going on in each different character's thoughts without having to be knowledgeable. A telepathic empath will also be able to study the needs of entities that are not in a feature to talk the equal. For instance, flora and animals. This paranormal capability of the telepathic empath makes it feasible for them to tell at the same time as a person is telling lies. They can effortlessly read the lies as they tumble up and down the person's mind. It is essential to word that someone can be a telepath and not continuously an empath. Where those requirements of telepathy and empathy intersect you have got a telepathic empath. On its personal telepathy is the functionality to look at minds. It is a concept that has been notably argued, with an same variety of proponents and opponents.

Psychometric Empath

Psychometric empaths are capable of choose out up electricity from inanimate gadgets together with garb. They can tell the feelings and critiques that a person went via without a doubt with the useful resource of touching an item of apparel previously worn through manner of that character. If you have got watched television suggests about missing dad and mom wherein psychics are contacted via the victim's family to attempt to find out what took place to that man or woman, you then definately most likely have watched a psychometric empath at work.

How are you able to inform if you are a psychometric empath? You will realize if you are a psychometric empath in case you discover yourself drawn or repelled through items based at the strength they emit. While different human beings are able to undergo existence now not affected by the use of things like chairs, scarves, cups and super inanimate gadgets, you may find out yourself hating the presence of these items in the event that they supply off horrible electricity. Of route, this could now not be the form of thing that you can effortlessly confide in people approximately. It would possibly seem bizarre to a colleague to inform them which you dislike the strength that the coffee maker offers or which you have become ordinary vibes from the photocopier. However, information which you aren't going crazy and that psychometric empathy is certainly actual have to deliver you some revel in of comfort.

Precognitive Empath

A precognitive empath has the capacity to enjoy an occasion earlier than it takes location. Often, this enjoy may be within the shape of a premonition or a strong foreboding. Precognitive empaths skilled a stunning shift in temper or bodily experience at the identical time as they may be undergoing the ones research. This should appear all through waking hours or in a dream. If you have ever had a terrible feeling that preceded a disaster or tragic occasion, then you definately professional a few factor this is referred to as precognition, which in wonderful phrases is what a precognitive empath goes thru on an almost every day foundation. This gift can be used to are watching for and beat back catastrophe, in particular while the empath takes time to exercising using their present. This present can also present itself undoubtedly. For instance, you can get an notion into a place you will be visiting to in the future, or the appearance of a new child toddler in the own family.

Chapter 3: Key Enemies Of An Empath

If you ever encounter an electricity vampire to your life, you will revel in it even in advance than you understand it. How so? Energy vampires have a manner of eliminating all the exact power from particular humans's lives and converting it with emotions of emotional drain. Some strength vampires try this intentionally, at the same time as others are unknowing about the destruction on account of their terrible energy and presence. Regardless of whether or not or now not or not an energy vampire is intentional or no longer, you should learn how to emerge as aware of one and a way to address being spherical one.

Let's begin with the aid of defining what an electricity vampire is. An energy vampire is a person that feeds off precise humans's energy. Often, an electricity vampire is an emotionally immature person who's no longer able to experience their non-public power voids and consequently appears to others for achievement. When someone this is emotionally mature and solid research sure emotions which embody anger or disappointment, they frequently try and technique the ones emotions thru themselves. Energy vampires do now not have this functionality. Instead of sifting via their feelings, they task those onto others. In the machine, they thieve away all of the proper power from others and replace it with their very very own feelings of anger, disappointment, melancholy, and distinct terrible feelings.

Dealing with an energy vampire may be quite draining, particularly when you are not aware about the reality that they will be an strength vampire. There can be generally whilst you will surprise why you continually revel in a particular shape of manner after spending time in the business enterprise business corporation of a powerful person. You can also additionally marvel whether or no longer or now not you're being unfair and judging that individual harshly. What you can no longer recognize is that you are proper to experience that manner due to the truth the character in question is an energy vampire who continuously manages to take you to the threshold of emotional exhaustion.

Energy vampires are to be had one of a type paperwork. Knowing how to tell them apart is step one in the direction of ensuring they're no longer able to stealing your emotional assets from you. The essential sorts of strength vampires, in any other case known as emotional vampires, are: the melodramatic vampire, the victim, the narcissist, the intimidator, judgmental, and the harmless vampires.

The Melodramatic Vampire

The melodramatic vampire feeds off drama. They can't exist in a place wherein there can be no drama. This kind of electricity vampire flourishes on blowing the whole thing out of share and want to normally be the primary individual in every display. If you're in a dating with this sort of character, you could constantly find out yourself caught up in a single public scene or each unique. Outbursts could be a common incidence and you could frequently capture yourself in cringeworthy public encounters. Melodramatic vampires do not care who receives swept up of their wave of battle and heightened emotion. They terrific care that they get the eye they need once they need it. At art work, a melodramatic vampire might also take the form of a colleague who is typically creating a big deal out of each little factor that they do. You will catch this colleague within the office kitchen and on the printer's complaining approximately how difficult their existence is due to one detail or any other. You could probable even pay hobby them whine on and on approximately how past due they were in getting home due to the truth a few distinct colleague did some issue that inconvenienced them, however minor that could were.

Why do melodramatic vampires behave this way? Most individuals who searching for hobby at some thing price accomplish that because it validates them. These are frequently the form of individuals who, for one purpose or the alternative, in no manner observed out a manner to be snug with their very own selves with out the want for outside validation. This will be due to being left out as a infant or because of the fact they grew up believing the arena revolves spherical them. Either manner, the kid also can increase up questioning that they are owed interest and that the first-rate way to experience entire is thru using making sure that the whole worldwide is looking them.

If you are faced with a drama queen or a melodramatic energy vampire, the first actual issue you want to understand is that this: you do now not owe genuinely all and sundry a while or interest. They are only a few humans in this Earth which you are obliged to offer your interest and time. Your kids, as an example, rank pretty at the listing of folks who can pretty name for to be made a problem on your existence. You also are well worth of the eye and time which you so effects deliver to others. Outside of these , you get to pick who gets it sluggish and who gets cut off.

A proper thing about individuals who love drama is that they may be smooth to discover. Soon after assembly a person, you may be in a function to inform whether or not or no longer they thrive on drama. You can spot it inside the manner they method struggle and the manner they create themselves in public. If someone is normally screaming and yelling and stressful to look the supervisor at each flip, run away and do no longer appearance back. This is the equal shape of man or woman so that you can burn the house and throw cooking pans at you due to the truth an antique acquaintance texted you at ten o'clock at night time time, without first identifying the reason for the text message.

If you are not able to walk a ways from someone that loves drama, for instance, if it's far a colleague or boss which you have to artwork with, the important element to don't forget is not to encourage their drama. Do no longer get tempted to take part in their shouting suits. Do not say things that feed their drama. As prolonged as a melodramatic vampire isn't getting some thing in cross back, they will not be capable of preserve up their show for too lengthy. The electricity they looking for will now not be to be had for them to scouse borrow. In the case of a family member who's a drama vampire, restrict the amount of time that you spend with them. Just due to the fact a person is associated with you does no longer suggest that they're allowed to get away with terrible behavior.

The Victim Vampire

The sufferer is constantly clean to choose out. They want to play the supporting feature in every terrible state of affairs of their lifestyles. They do no longer take responsibility for something and continuously have a finger organized to issue at someone else. An energy vampire that takes on the location of a sufferer can be identified with the useful useful resource of their love for proceedings and their entire loss of duty. In their international, nothing is ever their fault. Everyone else is to be blamed for their movements and they'll bitch approximately a few aspect and everything under the solar. Oh, and don't even problem dropping a while trying to get an apology out of them. They feed off the pity that they elicit from others each time they percent their woes. While it is critical to be sympathetic to the struggling of others, you have to be careful approximately the shape of interest which you display toward the sufferer. If you display too much sympathy, the victim will never leave you by myself. They will commonly maintain coming again in the desire that you will display them a number of this sympathy that they have gotten used to. Unlike the drama vampire that you can in all likelihood without difficulty cut off with out a 2nd perception, the sufferer is probably greater tough to put off. This is really because you may experience responsible about leaving at the back of someone who is in need of your assist but you should apprehend that those people want to take gain.

If the victim on your lifestyles is a person which you certainly care approximately, bear in thoughts assisting them set some dreams in their life which can make them sense as even though they may be on pinnacle of factors. Ensure that you mounted area measures of duty so that it will assist determine whether or not they'll be being accountable and operating within the path in their desires. For instance, if you have a sister this is constantly complaining approximately their charge variety, undergo in thoughts supporting them to set up a financial economic savings or funding account. Have them contribute a detail of their paycheck to this account each month. By doing this, you can have changed the narrative from truely one in every of pity to at least one wherein the victim feels empowered to do something about their existence.

Otherwise, if you have an power vampire in your life that likes to whine approximately everything, does now not take obligation for his or her non-public actions and that you aren't mainly invested in, experience free to lessen them out of your lifestyles. Limit the amount of time you spend spherical them and you'll start to experience your electricity stages peaking another time.

The Narcissist Vampire

Narcissism is a character infection this is characterised with the aid of an inflated revel in of self-importance, entitlement, and an obsession with one's bodily look. Narcissists take into account that they are the first-class issue given that sliced bread and could regularly go to first-rate lengths to show this detail. They do now not take kindly to grievance, and that they frequently do not care approximately what one in all a kind humans have to mention until it's miles said in admiration. Perhaps you've already encountered this kind of varieties of strength vampires into your life considering the truth that they love empaths.

Finding yourself in a courting, be it romantic or paintings, with a narcissist may be one of the most daunting things you could ever go through. You will spend your life placating the ego of the narcissist and saying sure to all their needs, even as your dreams fall on deaf ears. A narcissist will steal all the delight and air from a room and then blame you for it. They will want to manipulate each detail of your life and make it their very own vicinity.

Out of all strength vampires, the narcissist is probably the most dangerous primarily based at the lengths that they may be inclined to go to keep the repute quo. Because they may be incapable of feeling empathy, the narcissist will not even care that you are handling emotional drain because of them. They genuinely cannot relate on your trap 22 situation however lots you attempt to show them that you are getting crushed down by the use of their terrible energy.

When you discover your self confronted with someone who famous the capabilities of a narcissist vampire, the primary detail you have to do is recollect the possibility of reducing them out of your life. This might be clean in a few instances and tougher in others. For instance, if you are simply getting began on a romantic courting and be aware the symptoms of narcissism, it will possibly be much much less tough to transport away because you aren't invested. What takes vicinity at the same time as the signs and signs and symptoms begin showing up four years into a wedding? It might be more difficult to sincerely stroll away. It is even more tough while it is your boss who's the narcissistic vampire.

When dealing with a narcissistic boss, for example, you could want to be very clever about your approach. One of the things you can do is make sure which you by no means permit them to get under your pores and pores and skin. Do now not deliver the narcissist the pride of records that they will usually get a reaction out of you. This is what drives a narcissist—records that they may be able to push you to the issue in which you explode. If you in no way explode, you will have denied them the completing that they so yearn for. Another way to protect yourself is to avoid argument so that you in no manner deliver them a risk to curl your phrases toward you. Narcissists will take gain of each phrase that comes from your mouth to ensure that they have the top hand. As lengthy as you do no longer say some element, you'll have denied them the ammunition that they may be so determined to have.

Do no longer sense the pressure to massage your boss' ego certainly because of the truth they're a narcissist that prospers on it. It is tempting to play collectively with the narcissist handiest for the sake of preserving the peace. Many personnel brief examine that they may get favors from their boss through pronouncing the topics that their boss wants to pay attention. Always keep in mind which you had been hired due to the skills and charge which you deliver to the table, and also you do now not need to bounce to the track of your boss in reality as it makes him or her revel in better whilst you do. It isn't your system to appease the insecurities of your narcissistic boss due to the fact insecurities are in reality the premise motive of the narcissist's behavior.

What occurs then if the narcissist vampire to your life is someone that you love, or are romantically concerned in, or possibly even a family member? Loving a narcissist can be very draining, mainly because of the fact you frequently get now not anything in go back. Narcissists do not recognize a manner to love others. They love themselves and that they love the topics that one-of-a-kind humans do for them. They are also specialists at carrying down the folks who love them, mentally and emotionally just so they may be in no way able to come across their manipulative strategies.

If you are caught up in a relationship with a narcissist who is inclined to alternate (and this is very rare), don't forget going into professional counseling and establishing limitations that assist you preserve a healthy union.

If the narcissistic vampire on your existence is unwilling to alternate and is constantly abusive, walk away and do not appearance again. In many times, abusive narcissists most effective get worse, so do not stick round hoping that things gets better. You will nice be setting your self up for failure in case you refuse to prioritize your well-being, this is precisely what the narcissistic vampire is relying on.

For a extra widespread manual on information narcissists and the way to break out being in a courting with a narcissist, you can take a look at out my other e-book: Narcissism and Narcissistic Abuse Recovery: Free Yourself with the aid of Understanding the Narcissists Personality Disorder, What the Hell Happened in Your Relationship, and How to Effectively Heal.

The Intimidator Vampire

Have you ever met someone who behaved as though that they had a aspect to show? If you have spoke back positive to this query, then excessive chances are which you have encountered an intimidator vampire. Intimidator vampires have deep-seated insecurities that they constantly warfare with. They experience prone, small, and intimidated with the aid of using manner of existence and everything round them. They reiterate and compensate through way of in search of to make the people round them experience these gadgets in go again. As such, they're hell-bent on making others look inclined and inferior and unworthy. The intimidator vampire will regularly maintain bigoted views on topics, especially while this bigotry is shared internal a fixed that makes him anticipate he's better than he clearly is. Such vampires also are racist and could dedicate hate crimes in the direction of others, specifically on the equal time as in agencies. The biggest identifier of an intimidator vampire is the fact that they are now not capable of hold their very personal at the identical time as faced. They thrive thru hiding in the again of ridiculous ideals and in numbers. They can in no manner upward push up within the the front of a group of humans and say the topics they do until they have got the backing of their fellow bigots. You may be capable of spot an intimidator vampire primarily based on their loudmouth and regularly obnoxious conduct.

When coping with an intimidator vampire, the number one trouble you want to recognise is that their try and make you revel in inferior stems from their deep emotions of inferiority. They are not in fact as competitive and assured as they want to stumble upon. In the confines and protection in their homes, intimidator vampires are like scared little cats that need a hug. However, it isn't your pastime to provide this stage of consolation. Intimidator vampires also can want to benefit from expert counseling in case you need to confront their emotions of unworthiness. Another practical step to take while dealing with this vampire is to conform to disagree. Accept the reality that you could preserve divergent views with out moving into every other's faces approximately it. Do not attempt to argue with an intimidator vampire. They will beat you at it thru being loud and pronouncing the most outrageous things. Lastly, do no longer have interaction until you clearly have to. Whenever viable, walk away in advance than subjects boom. The intimidator vampire can in particular say very hurtful matters due to the fact they will be in search of to damage the ones spherical them. If you do no longer want to get caught up in this, virtually walk away and refuse to interact.

Judgmental Vampire

Why are some humans so judgmental? You probable realize some judgmental people in your life. They normally have some issue to mention about the whole thing, even though no man or woman has asked for their opinion. They will pick out apart one-of-a-type people's relationships, their preference of apparel, their manner of life picks, their career picks and all of these will fall short. It is often impossible to pride a judgmental character. Nothing you do will ever diploma as a bargain as their requirements. Having a judgmental spouse or determine can be specially discouraging, in particular whilst you are attempting your amazing to be the pleasant model of yourself.

So, once more, why are a few human beings so judgmental? To placed it succinctly, judgment often comes about because of what's indoors someone, and much less because of what goes on around them. It has been stated that we hate maximum in others the ones things that remind us of ourselves. This is the using strain inside the back of judgment. You won't even be acutely privy to it but the trauma which you enjoy will continuously be inside the again of your thoughts guiding your feelings and turning you into the judgmental individual which you said you'd in no way be.

Some human beings are often not capable to break up the movement from the doer, and as such will constantly have a finger to component even with out records the context of the act. When this is coupled with a lack of empathy, it could be specially difficult to be some element but judgmental.

If you've got had been given a judgmental vampire for your lifestyles, be cautious now not to take everything that they'll be pronouncing in my view. Understand that the jabs thrown your manner may also additionally genuinely be signs and symptoms of a few underlying harm that the vampire is managing. This does not advocate which you need to take everything mendacity down. Consider calling out the vampire on their conduct, but ever so sweetly so that it does now not become a shouting healthy. Being enterprise company and robust in your reality about who you're can also even assist to make certain which you aren't overly affected by the grievance of different people. If all else fails, lessen out the judgmental vampire out of your life. Life is honestly too short to paste round folks who are always seeking to located you down. Surround yourself with first rate electricity.

The Innocent or Unknowing Vampire

Some people drain us with out meaning to. They in reality come to us with their goals and issues because of the fact it's miles the only component they apprehend. Your kids, as an instance, will continuously flip to you for assist and reassurance without being aware of the reality that they drain you or that you want a person to guide and reassure you as nicely. Good buddies also can be the unknowing vampires in your lifestyles if they are continuously searching out to you to offer the emotional manual that can only come from a pal.

With the harmless vampire, it is important to remember that one of the only approaches of assisting someone is through showing them the way to treatment their non-public troubles. If your infant is always coming to you with the equal hassle, display them the manner to remedy it. Empower them just so they're an awful lot much less reliant on you. At the equal time, discover ways to make the effort out for yourself. Mothers, especially, have this overwhelming experience of guilt each time they test out of parenting for a few hours to have a while for themselves. Motherhood is a hard device and to do properly at it you may want to set apart moments in which you cognizance totally on your self-care, unapologetically and without a guilt. When it comes to your buddies, you may need to set obstacles and allow them to find out their private wings as properly. While it's far remarkable to be referred to as the friend that always indicates up for others, you furthermore may additionally need to show up for your self. This is the only way you will remain in appropriate form without feeling the consequences of being tired through the usage of the unknowing vampires to your lifestyles.

Signs of Emotional Exhaustion

The problem about emotional exhaustion, otherwise referred to as emotional drain, is that it could frequently be disguised as some thing else. For instance, you'll possibly enjoy emotional drain in the shape of headaches. When this happens, you'll be tempted to chalk it as tons as dehydration, exhaustion or simply the regular strain of your artwork. The truth is that emotional drain regularly creeps up on you, best at the way to understand eventually which you are really and certainly exhausted. You will try and look again and suppose decrease again to whilst the emotional drain began, and you can in all likelihood be not able to pinpoint the suitable 2nd. As an empath, you can experience each other character's terrible strength and the effect it has on you, and but be not able to consciously understand the cumulative results of that power. Just as you are sensitive to distinct human beings's wishes and emotional states, you could additionally need to be aware about your very personal desires and the state of your emotional health. Look out for the signs of emotional drain and take appropriate measures before it spirals out of control.

Insomnia/ Difficulty Falling Asleep

Insomnia is in all likelihood one of the loudest signs and symptoms of emotional exhaustion. When your thoughts is full of pressure and issues, it will become nearly now not feasible to doze off. The thoughts requires a sure u . S . Of calmness and relaxation just so it could settle right into a rustic this is conducive for sleep. An emotionally exhausted individual is at an area in which all of the emotion centers of their mind are fired up. They are like little flickering lighting that refuse to exit, although it's time for bed. Pay hobby to insomnia on the equal time as it comes calling. It is usually a clean signal that a few issue is incorrect on your existence. Nobody remains up at night time tossing and turning whilst they're emotionally healthy and satisfied of their life.

If you're having trouble drowsing, there are certain steps that you may take to make this a issue of the beyond. Of path, removing the stressors in your life (furthermore referred to as electricity vampires) have to be your bypass-to step each time you lure yourself falling down the black hollow this is emotional drain. However, we've were given to date decided that getting rid of electricity vampires isn't normally feasible relying on the kind of courting that we've got have been given with them. So, in the case of insomnia, there are numerous recommendations that you can follow to remedy the scenario.

First, discover ways to switch off from your assignment at the same time as you leave the place of work. Do no longer bring the stresses of one area to the following vicinity. By doing so, you will be allowing your self to hold all of the negative aura of the workplace environment and transfer it to your property, which must be your stable and satisfied place. Whenever viable, do now not convey your artwork domestic. Many personnel will lay unsleeping at night time involved approximately the pending document in their laptop with out knowing that their emotional fitness supersedes the importance of that report. Seriously, depart paintings at paintings and enjoy a while at home. You aren't what is protecting the company collectively. Your document isn't what will motive the agency to go returned crashing down. Learn to take existence for your very personal stride. If someone calls you after artwork hours for a few issue associated with paintings, make certain the cellphone name is brief and overlook about the trouble as rapid due to the fact the communication ends.

A enjoyable bathtub infused with important oils moreover does the trick in phrases of preventing insomnia. Water is a pal to an empath. Water cleanses all the dust and awful electricity of an empath and leaves them feeling invigorated and equipped for a non violent night time time of restful sleep. Couple this with a few chamomile tea and sleep meditation and you may be off to slumberland in advance than you understand it.

Lack of Motivation

When you began at your method, you had been complete of electricity and equipped to deal with any assignments coming your way. Three months down the road, you're struggling to evoke for the very technique you used to love. What changed? Well, you had numerous run-ins collectively with your supervisor who takes location to be a important narcissist. This manager has controlled to place on you down every step of the manner. They criticize your artwork, placed you down inside the the the front of others, and do now not appear to have a single type word to say about you. You have commenced out struggling collectively together with your self-esteem and might experience your voice becoming quieter and quieter, in which in advance than it became as soon as ambitious and confident. A lack of motivation is a smooth signal of emotional exhaustion. When you're constantly beat down emotionally it becomes almost not possible to be enthusiastic about topics anymore.

You will understand that your motivation has taken a achievement at the same time as the subjects that used to excite you start to experience like chores. Because your emotional power has been depleted, you have were given not whatever left to offer to the subjects that rely. Take a go searching you. How is your dwelling situation? Do you stay in a clean house? Do you're making your mattress whilst you awaken? Can you without a doubt say which you address yourself properly via taking care of your hygiene, your health, your healthy eating plan and a few issue else that relates to you? Were there days that you have dealt with yourself better? If certain, what modified? What are your dreams in life? Do you observe yourself installing the aware strive each day in the direction of the achievement of these dreams?

Taking inventory of your current instances, and what form of you've got contributed to those, is a extraordinary first step in the direction of identifying whether or not you're stimulated or now not. Intrinsic motivation is a hallmark of an emotionally sensible character. Emotional intelligence is a concept that an empath need to look at if they're trying to control those round them. The pinnacle information is that, as an empath, you already have the empathy part of emotional intelligence discovered out. You nice want to paintings at the possibility components, which embody motivating your self internally so you sincerely display up externally.

Anger and Irritability

When do you locate yourself most irritable and probable to snap on the smallest topics? More regularly than now not, you will be at risk of anger at the identical time as you're going thru a demanding occasion. When you're emotionally drained, you may no longer have the capacity for the staying electricity that is probably predicted from a ordinary and logical person. Small subjects that you can formerly have not noted will set you off and you will not be capable of hold your cool in conditions. Most humans are clever sufficient to recognize that anger comes from an area of worry, damage, or maybe frustration. These are all emotions that come approximately with emotional exhaustion. You'll in no manner see a happy character lashing out at some different. If you've got been brief-fused recently, endure in mind evaluating whether or not or no longer or not you have additionally been going through a second of emotional turmoil. You are probably not an irritated character but without a doubt a super individual who had been given driven too a long manner and for too prolonged.

Detachment

What takes region to an empath who has been subjected to torrents of emotional abuse by using the usage of the power vampires of their life? They studies to influence smooth, and with this guidance easy comes a revel in of detachment. Being pushed to the element of emotional drain is a shape of trauma, and trauma often breeds coping strategies. Emotional detachment is a shape of coping approach. A character that is emotionally indifferent will battle to form connections because of the reality they've unknowingly switched off their emotions to protect themselves.

Detachment may be towards people or perhaps in the direction of your very personal passions. You might in all likelihood find yourself feeling no desire or hobby in a particular topic that previously excited you, without a doubt because of the fact you're protecting yourself from the heartbreak and emotional fatigue of failure. You might also additionally subconsciously pick out out to distance your self from humans because of the truth you have were given faced emotional exhaustion whenever you get close to a person.

Pay interest any time you begin to revel in as in case you are going numb wherein emotions are worried. This is your be-careful call that a few element is not right.

Nobody turned into imagined to go through existence no longer feeling any experience of pleasure or happiness from something. If you capture yourself feeling numb and unexcitable approximately things, communicate to a person. You might be completely worn-out and uninterested in putting up a fight. Professional assist or maybe a kind listening ear truly may additionally offer you with the jumpstart you need to begin feeling over again. And preserve in mind, if the emotional drain that brought about you to begin feeling honestly detached and numb comes from some thing that you do no longer must have on your lifestyles, kick the stressor out. This consists of your task. There isn't always any paycheck on this Earth that is surely really worth your emotional fitness.

Physical Pains

Emotional drain occasionally suggests up inside the shape of physical pain. There are some inform-tale physical signs and symptoms and symptoms that recommend that someone is within the throes of burnout. These embody constant inexplicable headaches or migraines or even dizziness. You might even start to experience shortness of breath and coronary heart palpitations. All the ones physical symptoms and signs and symptoms and signs factor to an underlying problem of emotional fatigue and possible anxiety, that is every a symptom and a cease result of emotional drain. When confronted with physical pain, your first save you should be your medical doctor's place of job. This will help you confirm that there isn't always some thing bodily incorrect with you. If that is the case, then you may skip without delay to the subsequent step of identifying all the strength vampires which have pushed you to the element of emotional drain. Most medical docs will no longer pull away from giving their honest evaluation of the state of affairs, particularly when they apprehend that there may be no bodily reason to your signs and symptoms. Many physicians are well aware about the tribulations that a whole lot of people go through of their regular lives and are able to perceive the signs of emotional drain from a mile off.

Lots of Crying

Granted, empaths are probably to cry masses. There is constantly a few component ready throughout the corner to tug at their heartstrings. It may be a adorable video of a kitten or a child taking their first steps and the empath will locate themselves triumph over with emotion. Being considerably emotional is the empath's giveaway. However, in case you suddenly find your self bursting into tears within the center of the day approximately not anything especially, you is probably going through emotional drain.

Crying is a top notch element. A correct properly-timed cry can be pretty restoration. A happy cry, alternatively, is constantly welcome and seldom makes all and sundry uncomfortable. However, if you are spontaneously crying inside the center of the day, within the subway, at art work, at some point of lunch or even as you are printing your reports, you then in reality can also need to take a seat down down and take inventory of your emotional fitness. There is a few technology inside the lower returned of crying: while a person is experiencing sturdy and overwhelming feelings, be that of disappointment or pride, the limbic device options up those emotions and sends a sign to the autonomic apprehensive device. In return, the worried system activates the tear glands, or activates the waterworks if you want, ensuing in a extremely good cry. An emotionally drained character is in a country of exceptional emotional duress. They will undergo their day experiencing incredibly strong feelings due to the fact they're absolutely worn out. Your limbic tool does no longer realize that you are in the center of a assembly, so it will simply pick out up on the ones emotions and then deliver the crucial symptoms to the annoying system.

Hopelessness

A first rate singer as soon as asked, in which do broken hearts bypass? A top rejoinder to that question might be, in which do hopeless minds pass? Hope is the fireside that keeps you shifting even on the equal time as you aren't positive of techniques the following day may be. Can you enjoy that fireplace for your stomach proper now? If not, what came about to that hearth? What took it away?

In the face of emotional exhaustion, it is able to be now not viable to enjoy hopeful about a few problem. The mind is a effective organ. In fact, the thoughts is the most powerful organ and device that a person possesses. In your thoughts, you could conceive mind and decide what you need to be. You can triumph over tribulations virtually with the resource of telling your mind that you'll. Many people have come to be remarkable and left lasting legacies in reality due to the fact they positioned their thoughts to it. There isn't always a few thing that you can not do even as your thoughts is in a incredible location. Hopelessness stems from a mind this is in a terrible region. When your thoughts and emotion had been corrupted by the use of the terrible energies of energy vampires, you discover your self stuck with a large simple of darkness and hopelessness. Everywhere you appearance appears bleak. Your goals do now not take into account. Your suffering appears countless. You do not have desire that the next day may be higher than these days. You can not see a way out. Narcissists are specially extremely good at pushing their victims in the direction of hopelessness because they apprehend that that may be a certainly effective way of shackling a person to their popularity quo. A narcissist vampire will continuously will let you apprehend that there may be no lifestyles past your current-day situations. They will let you know that there's no better mission than the one you've got got (if they may be your boss) and that there may be no man or woman who can also need to ever love you in case you depart them (if they'll be your associate). The critical issue is to understand the ones statements due to the fact the blatant lies that they are. These lies are designed to get you feeling hopeless so you'll be with out difficulty worn down and made to do precisely as an energy vampire desires you to do.

Chapter 4: Thriving As A Psychic Empath

If you are an empath who wants to take all over again control on your lifestyles, you may be pleased to recognize that there are some short-time period techniques that you can use. These are matters that you can do on your regular lifestyles, beginning now, to experience higher and be extra on top of factors of your power.

Learn to Say No and Walk Away

One of the most effective tips to managing your strength area as an empath is reading to say "No" and on foot away whilst horrific energy enters your location. In your regular life and interactions, there can be instances in that you start to sense your strength draining away. For example, you might be in an environment wherein argumentative colleagues are beginning to muddle your place with terrible energy. At this element, it's far tremendous to stroll away and take away yourself from that environment. It is important to perform that without being apologetic. As an empath, you're often involved approximately offending one among a type humans. The problem with this kind of mind-set is that it locations you in unpleasant conditions as a substitute. When strolling far from a poisonous situation, achieve this with out feeling the want to make an apology and without worrying approximately who gets irritated. Unapologetically protecting your power is important.

Just Breathe

At this issue within the e-book, we've got were given already determined that empaths generally generally tend to hate crowds. So, what takes vicinity at the same time as you discover your self in a situation wherein being part of a crowd is inevitable? If you can not avoid a situation that calls for a meeting of a massive group of humans, then make sure you function your self in a manner wherein you're at the bottom threat of emotional drain. Standing within the middle of a crowd pleasant makes you specially liable to energy drain from the energy vampires surrounding you from all components. A extra stable function will be at the threshold of the group, someplace in a corner in which some bits of you are in component hidden from the electricity indicators coming from the gang.

Breathing deeply is but every other way an empath can address their feelings after they start to experience crushed. A deep breath can center and ground you even as you begin to revel in tired and bombarded thru the first-rate strength signs which you acquire from those round you. A deep exhale from the mouth serves to expel the terrible energy from internal you, at the equal time as an inhale through the nose replaces this with the easy strength from nature. Breathing inner and out is also a meditation trick this is geared closer to assisting you end up more aware of your emotions. A deep breath can calm your nerves and put off anger in a direct. Next time someone is projecting their anger onto you, take a brief breath and permit your self to experience the fine strength taking center stage for your body.

Limit Physical Contact

As a psychic empath, you are capable of acquire the strength of the human beings around you through eye touch or even physical touch. This manner that the greater you touch and have interaction with human beings, the much more likely you're to get maintain of the strength that they have interior them. As plenty as feasible, restriction the quantity of bodily contact which you allow on your life, at least until you're advantageous that you could no longer be receiving horrific energy from a selected man or woman. It is inside your rights as someone to refuse to offer hugs to strangers or maybe unique friends and buddies, mainly if the ones people make you sense tired after each hug. Sometimes, even the most nicely-because of this people can drain your strength via physical contact if they'll be needy and constantly looking for physical affection and affirmation. Stay-at-home moms who spend all day with small children who're constantly clawing at them to be picked up and tended to recognize how draining it can be to continually be on the giving end for bodily affection. At the surrender of the day, such mothers exceptional want to be left on my own with none physical touch. Empaths typically commonly tend to have the equal problem with regards to steady physical touch. In the equal breath, reenergizing bodily contact can be very effective to the empath. An empath should; consequently, discern out the folks that are outstanding for hugging and people that must be prevented.

Make Time for Alone Time

Creating by myself time is some different crucial method that an empath should have if they're to stay to inform the tale residing in a crowded global in which escaping other humans's energies is sort of impossible. Alone time is one of the first-rate techniques to fully recharge and get organized to stand another day for the empath. During this on my own time, you could pick out to perform a little thing makes you satisfied. You can look at a e-book or watch a healthy film. You may additionally even take a snooze or soak in a bubble bath. The excellent man or woman who must make the rules of by myself time is you, counting on what you want notable. However, the critical element component to think about is that alone time collectively together with your smartphone does now not depend as by myself time. The telephone is one of the top enemies of an empath. Not only do smartphones intervene with the functionality to sleep thanks to their blue moderate, they may be moreover awash with depressing records and social media trolls who rank distinctly as power vampires. Always hold in mind to area your cellular phone onto plane mode in advance than going into by myself time. Calls and text messages want to now not be responded, at the equal time as you're playing your solitude. Any emails that come thru throughout your 2d of peace should remain unanswered. Learning to replace off and honestly bask in the quiet is one of the finest offers you can ever deliver your self as an empath.

Say Goodbye to TV and Facebook

Another super tactic on the way to help on your survival as an empath is switching off the television and staying off the Internet. The television and the Internet are each brilliant channels for getting access to records. Unfortunately, they will be frequently packed with some of terrible electricity that can be debilitating for the empath that soaks everything in. While it is probably beneficial to study television and get proper of access to the Internet every now and again, it's far very easy to over-devour inappropriate records and going overboard is only going to place on you down. A top way to transport approximately that is to set aside time for having access to the internet and TV. This permits you to reveal the type of facts that is being despatched your way and placed an stop to topics whilst you begin to revel in tired. Staying off social media is likewise an first-rate concept. Facebook, Instagram, Snapchat and exceptional social media structures assist us stay related to our friends and family however are also notably negative while abused. If you are able to name the people you need at the smartphone and speak to them, then there absolutely isn't always any need to have severa social media pages that disclose you to the negativity of the net community.

Prioritize Yourself

As an empath, it's miles ordinary and natural to constantly placed the dreams of others earlier of yours. You are born to be a giver. It is part of who you're. In truth, giving is the essence of who you are. To continue to exist in a global that is almost constantly taking with out giving something in circulate again you will want to discover ways to be selfish. It is ok to place yourself first. In fact, in line with airline safety commands you are speculated to placed on the oxygen masks first in advance than attempting to help others. In ordinary lifestyles, this means that you ought to constantly address yourself first earlier than searching after others. This makes best experience as you can't pour from an empty cup. Train your self to prioritize your self first. It is good enough to fear approximately yourself first and to care about your self first earlier than being involved about the following individual. You would possibly revel in guilty for a while, but you can soon comprehend that you are in a higher function to offer to others when you supply to your self first.

Visualization for Protection

Visualization is the art work of taking your mind on an adventure. Instead of simply considering your modern-day surroundings, visualization lets in you to take away yourself from that state and think about a few detail plenty higher. A proper manner to utilize visualization in shielding your power is to count on yourself encased with the aid of an impenetrable defend that protects you from all the lousy power of the region. You might also need to even visualize a fierce lioness guarding your private area and walking off all power vampires. This approach comes in to be had whilst you suddenly comprehend you're within the presence of an strength vampire, specially the innocent vampire. With the harmless vampire, you'll be halfway proper proper into a communique earlier than you comprehend how invested you're and the manner drained you experience. This is a extremely good time to apply visualization to protect and regain your energy and save you truly making an funding in the verbal exchange.

Be Grateful for Your Gift

Empathy is a notable issue. It isn't always a burden that you have been cursed with. Being an empath is a exquisite present that has been bestowed on you so that you can heal your self and others. When you are within the trenches dealing with heavy feelings, empathy can experience just like the worst trouble to have. You can also have days at the equal time as you preference you weren't able to feeling as you do. There can be moments even as you may be green with envy of your a good buy plenty much less empathetic friends, and their capability to shrug off matters and occasions as if they did not arise. Even inside the ones moments, bear in mind which you are substantially blessed and pretty gifted. Gratitude is a superb way to teach your thoughts to peer your empathy as an excellent aspect in desire to a heavy burden.

Psychologists have studied the human mind and determined that being thankful has a manner of lifting depressed spirits. In reality, folks who are often coping with depression are informed to write down down down three matters that they are thankful for each day. After several weeks of constantly expressing gratitude, most humans document happier and lighter spirits. If your spirit is heavy approximately the truth which you are an empath, recollect maintaining a pocket e book wherein you could write down 3 matters that you are grateful for every day. It can be the fact that your intuition saved you from doing a little factor or the way you've got been able to convey a person else's spirits at paintings. Either way, you will quickly start to realize that what you've got were given is a good problem that ought to be cherished, regardless of the way it feels on a few days.

Consume Positive Material

Being an empath can be tough at times and the fastest path to becoming a psychic empath warrior is to indulge inside the worldwide of self-improvement. Whilst there may be an extraordinary quantity of useless data accessible, there may be additionally a plethora of exceptional information available in the form of books and audiobooks. A e-book can be a worthwhile accomplice even as you're suffering with an unruly mind because it engages your interest on a trendy set of thoughts or capabilities a first-rate way to analyze. And even if you do no longer like analyzing, you can despite the fact that take pleasure in a brilliant audiobook in your pass to and fro to or from paintings. Audiobooks are especially extraordinary in making sure that you do no longer wander off on your personal thoughts, as you have got a person proper there studying to you, making sure you do no longer song out and visit that quiet region that empaths need to retreat to. As you continue to study new statistics over the years, you may be amazed at how loads of an impact this can have on your life.

Chapter 5: Long-Term Survival Strategies

As an empath, you can need lengthy-term survival techniques that will help you cope with residing in a global this is fairly disturbing and whole of negative energy with out getting crushed. Unlike the shorter-time period strategies which have been discussed in Chapter four, the lengthy-term techniques will require a chunk little bit of practice and staying power. Incorporating those strategies for your everyday lifestyles will help you switch out to be a better character who can deal with themselves and impact the sector spherical you without dropping yourself. And don't worry, a few people would in all likelihood say that you are changing, that you are becoming greater selfish and inaccessible or that they do not recognize who you are anymore. Do no longer take the ones statements too significantly. Part of growth is discarding the vintage bits approximately us that now not artwork for us and bringing onboard new tactics that assist us come to be the fantastic variations of ourselves.

Define Your Needs as a Person

One of the very first matters you can want to do is outline what your wishes and goals are as a person or ladies. Every person has what they receive as true with to be their reason and purpose in lifestyles. For instance, your present day cause and objective is probably to be the wonderful mom on your toddler. Maybe you're set on engaging in severa milestones as an employee and getting beforehand in your profession. Your intention may be in truth to be as glad and happy as is humanly viable. The most important problem to do is to be clean on what this very critical want is to your existence. Remember you are allowed to have a couple of wishes and categorize all of them as a challenge. Now the following issue after figuring out your goals is to decide the topics that you require to be able to meet these goals. For instance, a mother who desires to do the incredible thru using their infant may moreover require a supportive partner with a view with the intention to balance the demands of parenting and having a career. Such a mom may be uncompromising in their choice of accomplice. They will now not permit a accomplice that is non-supportive and strength-sapping anywhere near them. This is due to the reality they have got already defined and characteristic a smooth photograph of what their goals are.

This type of mind-set can also workout to the place of business. If you haven't decided what you want and what you gained't stand for, you could frequently find out yourself surrounded thru the same energy vampires that you're attempting your exceptional to keep away from. Defining your desires as an worker will help you decide what employer to paintings for in terms of business enterprise commercial enterprise agency subculture, profession improvement, and reimbursement goals amongst others. A commonplace trouble that empaths have isn't records at the same time as to speak up. As extended as what your needs are, you will be in a feature to talk up. When you are pushed to the wall you'll be very clear approximately what's taking area and take steps to exchange the state of affairs due to the truth you are already familiar on the facet of your desires.

Take out a pocket e-book proper now and make a listing of the topics that you want from life. Take time to search your soul and discern out precisely what you will need from life if it changed into as an awful lot as you. Now take a step lower back and recognize that it's miles all as a whole lot as you. Only you may determine what you get from existence relying on the belongings you allow to occur. Use your pocket e book of needs and desires to remind yourself of what you are hoping to get out of existence each time you start to enjoy muddled or depleted. If someone is responsible for making you experience muddled or depleted, remind yourself that this person isn't appearing in the amazing hobby of your desires after which do away with them out of your lifestyles.

Stamp Boundaries in Your Life

In the begin, empaths are seemed to have very inclined boundaries and is some aspect the empath need to consciously paintings on to decorate. Defining your desires will supply you to the very critical 2d step of stamping obstacles and boundaries. Stamping limitations in your lifestyles lets in others to recognize what you may tolerate and what you won't tolerate. When you have got obstacles, you train distinct people the manner to cope with you.

Many of the humans which you first of all meet do not understand the way to deal with you and depend on the cues you supply them to make experience of for themselves. Sure enough, there are some written common decency guidelines that govern social interactions. For instance, it's far impolite to invite out a lady at the same time as she is out and about alongside facet her husband. Almost anyone is aware about this. Those who do no longer but understand this may soon discover and in a totally ugly way. However, there are first rate non-public guidelines that you could have that human beings do now not realize of. Let's say as an example that you have set apart an hour earlier than bedtime to meditate. The colleagues you determine with do now not realize this, so that they keep calling you prolonged once you've left the administrative center to speak about paintings. Some of them call even as you're within the center of meditation. Meditation is your steady region and it slow to recharge. Instead of being disappointed about your colleagues calling and retaining quiet about it, placing boundaries could appear like this: Your colleague calls proper earlier than bedtime, you refuse to pick out out the selection. The subsequent morning you permit them to with courtesy realize that your evenings are set aside for own family time and private time. Chances are that they will now not be calling you after art work anymore.

Boundaries do no longer clearly exercise to colleagues. You need to set obstacles together along with your family and pals too. While maximum parents love our buddies and households, it's far crucial to understand that further they will be very draining of their desires. When faced with an empath, some friends and family can take and take till there can be no longer some thing left to take. As an empath, you want to apprehend that you may love someone and despite the fact that say "no" to them if saying "yes" might be negative to you. Whether we're speaking approximately pronouncing yes whenever a member of the family dreams a person to babysit or announcing certain to requests for price range and soft loans, you need to be cautious to draw the boundaries wherein they belong. After a while, human beings will recognise that there are things that you may not permit for your existence and could save you inquiring for favors at every flip. By doing this, you will be able to live a miles happier lifestyles as you are on pinnacle of things of methods you need to stay your life and not letting others manipulate you.

Take Note of the Energy Drainers and Energizers

In order to favorably impose your barriers and barriers, it's far going to be critical to define the electricity drainers and energizers for your life. Just as there are strength vampires that eliminate from you, there are people and conditions that serve to enhance your electricity and morale. As a touchy person, your energizers are property that ought to be guarded. Long walks, by myself time, communing with nature, and splendid time spent with a person who virtually loves you are all examples of energizers that an empath will gain from. Once you understand what steals your delight and what adds to it, you may be capable of draw the lines regarding wherein every of them suits to your existence.

Balance Your Chakras

Do you apprehend what chakras are? According to Indian spiritual notion, chakras are the energy elements that every character is born with. Every individual has a whole of seven chakras, which begin right at the start of the backbone and pass all the way as a whole lot because the top of the top. The seven chakras are responsible for reenergizing you in various factors of your lifestyles. For example, the solar plexus chakra, moreover referred to as Manipura, is what offers you your self-identity and self warranty. If your sun plexus chakra is underactive, you will war to make enjoy of who you're or even lack in vanity. If it's miles overactive, you would in all likelihood emerge as being egotistical or conceited. Whether you ascribe to those ideals or not, it is crucial to well known that the idea of the chakras is one that makes wellknown sense. As humans, we aren't really empty vessels that emerge as after which complete our journeys in mortality. There is a riding pressure in the lower returned of our movements and our lives. As an empath, it's far important to make certain that you balance your chakras (or whatever you could opt for to call them) so you must have a balanced lifestyles.

There are severa smooth pointers that you can examine in your lifestyles to make certain which you wake up your chakras to help you be the satisfactory model of yourself. Walking barefoot, for example, is understood to attach you with the earth in what is called grounding. In religious circles, grounding is the relationship that occurs amongst your self as a non secular character and the earth with all its power. Grounding permits you to launch all of the bad power that is pent up internal of you whilst getting some nicely energy from the earth in move returned. The chakra accountable for maintaining you grounded to the strength of the earth is referred to as the inspiration chakra. Grounding is crucial for empaths who locate themselves stuck in their head an excessive amount of overthinking and overanalyzing.

Getting a calming rubdown and dancing are one-of-a-type methods you could stir up your chakras and heal yourself when you have been feeling a piece beaten. If you do not have the time or opportunity for both, soak your self in a warm temperature bathtub whole with tub salts. Epsom salts combined with lavender oil make for a completely relaxing and energizing tub an amazing manner to have you ever ever ever feeling reborn and absolutely balanced. While you're soaking in your bath, name first-rate mind into your thoughts with the aid of using repeating affirmations together with I am loved, I am constant, I am sturdy.

Strengthen Your Mind with Positive Affirmations

Speaking of affirmations, that's a few extraordinary detail that you'll want to investigate as a long-term approach if you want to take control of your existence as an empath. Positive affirmations serve to enhance the empath's subconscious mind of who they actually are, what they consider and the way they need to stay their existence.

For every one, as a more youthful infant, the subconscious mind is form of a sponge. No count number number what is inside the environment, incredible or terrible, favorable or unfavorable, the sub-conscious thoughts will absorb it. So anything terrible developments and beliefs your parents have, it's miles most probable you picked up those undesirable inclinations and ideals. And for the touchy empath, the probabilities of absorbing these damaging beliefs and tendencies are a first rate deal better.

This is why self-interest is so essential, due to the fact we're in a position to test the unwanted and make a aware attempt to dispose of this and reprogram our subconscious mind. Through the usage of repetitive splendid affirmations over an prolonged time body we're capable of rewire the subconscious mind to create a much greater appropriate existence, and may then help others to do the identical.

Positive affirmations may be a few difficulty which you need them to be, as long as they may be high quality and encourage you to be your extraordinary self.

Example of awesome affirmations that you could paintings with include:

I am an empowered empath.

I am a non violent and peaceful person.

I am clever and make sensible picks.

I certainly have the power and realize-a way to alternate my life.

I am no longer a prisoner of my errors.

I lure wealth and abundance into my lifestyles.

I surround myself with excellent and uplifting power.

Another thing to phrase with first rate affirmations is that you could moreover use them to carry a few thing into your existence that you do now not currently have but need to hold in your life. However, on the identical time as you verify this appropriate element, you need to deliver it into the triumphing second with the aid of talking as in case you have already got it.

You do not need to affirm "I want." By asserting "I need" you're emitting the vibration "I need" and are simplest going to collect decrease again the vibration of "I need" therefore, you could never without a doubt display up this preference. By emitting the vibration "I am" or "I in reality have" this is the vibration you may accumulate and in the end the manner you get up what you actually preference, with the aid of the usage of putting forward as if you have already were given it.

For instance, permit's say you desire a black Range Rover.

You may want to verify: "I energy a stunning black Range Rover." And as you verify this desire, use the power of visualization and certainly experience yourself gripping the steering wheel of the Black Range Rover with the brown leather interior the use of down the road. Feel yourself within the second.

A terrific example of a splendid manifestation is Jim Carey writing himself a take a look at for 10 million dollars to himself dated 10 years into the future, retaining it in his pockets. And after nearly 10 years have become up, he found that he turn out to be going to earn 10 million dollars for appearing in the movie Dumb and Dumber. Amazing!

Make a listing of the matters that you need to confirm and lure right now after which use them as your affirmations to strengthen your mind and your reality. I would advise then getting yourself an affirmation magazine, so you have something organized to jot down down down and maintain all of your affirmations. You can undergo your affirmations every first detail inside the morning or proper earlier than you go to mattress.

Express Gratitude

What might be a high-quality addition proper subsequent in your affirmation magazine is a gratitude magazine.

Affirmations and expressing gratitude tie in thoroughly together and I endorse filling out every journals together. Let me give an reason behind why.

While you are someone that consists of an first-rate and admirable capability to discover one-of-a-type humans's ache and produce them recovery, you want to always bear in mind that you are the vessel thru which the power of the universe flows. Remaining humble inside the face of the winning which you have been bestowed with is a great way of making sure that this gift continues to flourish. Arrogance has been acknowledged to face inside the way of many success reminiscences. Do not allow yours be one in each of them. Always take a couple of minutes of it gradual each day to express gratitude for what you're capable of doing. Expressing gratitude for your lifestyles serves functions. One is that it lets you start seeing your functionality due to the truth the gift that it's far, and no longer as a burden which you have been yoked with. The 2d reason gratitude serves is that while you vibrate on the frequency of gratitude, you'll acquire extra matters for your life to be glad approximately, as this is the vibration you are emitting.

Here are a few examples of gratitude statements to get your mind ticking:

I am grateful for the life and enjoy of lifestyles.

I am thankful for my health.

I am thankful for my buddies and circle of relatives.

I am thankful for my secure haven, apparel, meals, and water.

I am grateful for the internet and being able to hook up with my buddy internationally.

I am thankful for my lovely pets. They carry me lots pleasure to my lifestyles.

Can you already see the power of running towards gratitude? After paying attention to those statements of gratitude your thoughts already starts offevolved to experience more powerful and you start to feel good about yourself. So many human beings whinge and attention on what they DO NOT have and preserve to vibrate on the frequency of lack! And what do you watched they keep to receive...? More Lack!

Gratitude is notably powerful and noticeably suggest your exercising it in case you need to change your existence in a immoderate incredible manner.

Just much like the confirmation journal, I may want to suggest making an investment in a gratitude mag, so you have a few factor neat and organized to fill out every day, both first element inside the morning or truely in advance than you go to sleep. This will keep you responsible and you will be able to mirror again in time and phrase the adjustments this easy interest has needed to your lifestyles.

Listen in your Body!

It isn't always hard for an Empath to be in tune with their body. They apprehend at the same time as a meal makes them experience properly and they understand while a meal makes them experience sick. The problem is while you select out to disregard this feel. Despite being able to be in song with their frame in the occasion that they want to, empaths are liable to using meals as an get away from their annoying lifestyles. However, doing this for an extended time frame will most effective bring about shame and guilt so it is vital to live in track at the side of your frame and simplest consume what makes you sense appropriate after. Yes, the oily Chinese meal may additionally taste proper on the time, but you apprehend straight away even as you're going to revel in like crap after and remorse it.

If you're usually ingesting fast meals, you'll have a more difficult time stepping into touch together with your inner and satisfactory self in comparison to someone who chooses to eat a nicely-balanced weight loss program of protein, low-GI carbohydrates, and healthy fat. Respect all 3 macronutrients as each plays an critical function in serving the frame.

Additionally, make certain you get plenty of water to drink. Water flushes out pollution from the frame and leaves you feeling hydrated and refreshed. The benefits of water may additionally be seen at the pores and skin. You can flow into from breakout-inclined pores and pores and pores and skin to sparkling pores and pores and skin in a rely of weeks in case you keep up your water intake. If water can do such wonders to the pores and pores and skin (it in reality is seen for all to look), agree with what it does on the inner. Water cleanses you from the inner out. It isn't always any wonder that most empaths love water. Whether they're eating it, swimming in it or taking a tub, most empaths swear by way of way of the cleansing and healing powers of water.

Meditation and Yoga

Pencil in meditation in your time table and you'll start to have a look at your self turning into extra aware of your emotional and highbrow states. Meditation lets you do away with the clutter in your life on the identical time as channeling in the acceptable electricity and focusing on the immoderate first-rate. A extremely good hassle about meditation is that there are numerous assets which can be available on the Internet for free of charge to be able to will let you get better at meditating. You may moreover select out to get proper of get right of entry to to to YouTube channels which are committed to meditation or perhaps download meditation apps from the app shops. Whichever manner you bypass about it, you could rapid be aware that you can have an improved enhance of electricity and could enjoy calmer, greater comfortable, and less irritable.

Yoga additionally serves a instead comparable motive. Having been in existence for over five thousand years, Yoga has been used specially as a way of connecting to the better power of the Universe. The particular purpose of Yoga become to sell self-focus and discernment in humans and motive them to look wherein they stood inside the simple big picture of the Universe.

Create Your Safe Place

This might be the most crucial method the empath can implement of their lifestyles. Every empath requires a place this is free from the everyday distractions in which they can retreat and recharge on the stop of the day and be by myself with their thoughts. It is vital that you create a bodily place in that you revel in in truth strong and in that you do not need to engage with absolutely each person which you don't want to. Your steady location can be your very own bed room or perhaps a eating place that has a nook income region in which you could cover faraway from absolutely everyone else. While for your secure place, make certain you switch off your cell smartphone and your thoughts as properly simply so the worries of the outside worldwide do no longer interrupt your 2d of relaxation. Bring a notepad and pen with you and write down your thoughts, mind, dreams, and objectives.

Chapter 6: Owning Your Superpowers

Being an empath does not ought to be a fight towards steady suffering and emotional drain. As an empath, you have got were given a effective gift that you can harness to make the sector a better area. The capability to revel in power isn't always something that everyone has. As a rely of truth, studies has shown that simplest about 20% of the arena are categorized as substantially touchy, a label under which empaths loosely fall.

Furthermore, about three% of the complete population qualifies as having a psychic empathic potential. What this suggests is which you are a minority in the global, but you may despite the fact that use your competencies to effect the rest of the arena in a big way. Sometimes you do loads in reality via specializing in the ones closest to you. Someone smart as quickly as said; be the change you need to appearance inside the international. As you're making the aware try to art work on your weaknesses and grow to be the awesome model of yourself, you unconsciously supply others permission to do the identical.

Top Superpowers of Every Psychic Empath

You are likely questioning whether or no longer the best issue you may ever be accurate at is sensing emotion and feeling the ache of others. On the surface, it may seem like this is all there can be to a psychic empath. Fortunately, this is not the case. Empaths are proficient with extremely good superpowers that they might use to do appropriate within the global. If this comes as a surprise to you, then it is probably due to the reality you have been riddled with self-doubt now not capable of be aware the wonderful aspects on your present. Let's explore the superpowers of the psychic empath.

The Superpower of Vision and Discernment

When a psychic empath settles their thoughts and learns to paintings thru the litter of their everyday existence, they might gain a imaginative and prescient that everyday human beings are not able to. This is because such an empath is able to sift through the chaff and pick out the critical facts. Empaths have a three-sixty diploma view on subjects, and because of this, they are capable of make surprisingly visionary and discerning leaders. Of course, such an empath may additionally should paintings via their everyday lack of enthusiasm for management roles. When a willing empath takes on a management role, there is usually a change for the better. They can observe the humans that they may be fundamental properly, expect their desires and hooked up area measures to cater for those dreams. Because they may be brilliant listeners, empaths make human beings revel in heard and listened to, that is a key excellent of an exemplary chief.

The Superpower of Advanced Intuition

While other people struggle to pay attention their intestine instinct genuinely, the empath's intuition leaves not something to hazard; it's miles loud, easy and wishes to be heard. In many cases, the simplest cause why an empath might probable fail to facet with their instinct is because of the reality they determined on to disregard it, now not because it did not display up at the identical time as required. A psychic empath's instinct is form of a nicely-skilled military with crimson flags which may be hoisted whenever there is drawing near hazard. This military works tirelessly and nonstop. A psychic empath that permits their army to flourish will without difficulty will allow you to apprehend that your new associate isn't any suitable for you, even whilst you suppose you are madly in love with this character. Just via searching at a person, an empath can inform while that person has specific intentions or in any other case.

Empaths who do not forget their advanced intuition are able to avoid a whole lot of unstable conditions.

Additionally, the psychic empath can also use their superior instinct in phrases of creating hard picks. They are able to use this present to vividly sift through the array of options which is probably supplied to them and in the long run decide which unique choice resonates with them terrific.

The Superpower of Psychic Ability

Seeing that this ebook is known as Psychic Empath Warrior, it might be wrong for the empath's superpower of psychic capacity to be lacking from this list. The empath's psychic capability permits them to appearance matters in advance than they take location or even at the same time as they'll be taking place even though they will be separated thru lots of miles from the actual event. An empath's psychic capacity will allow them to revel in the pain of a loved one who's present manner a hurtful situation masses of miles away. Have you ever stuck your self thinking about someone unexpectedly and at the same time as you call them, they assist you to understand that they've been going thru a difficult time? This may be because of your psychic functionality. Your nature as an empath will preserve you related to this individual who's continents away, on the equal time as your psychic functionality lets in you to obtain signs, inside the equal manner, that a distraught man or woman would possibly supply SOS messages inside the desire of being rescued. Further down in this bankruptcy, there can be a detailed exploration of the topics that you can encompass on your every day lifestyles to develop your psychic capability and make it higher than it already is.

The Superpower of Healing

Whether they're healing with the aid of way of using speaking existence into others or without a doubt with the resource of surrounding others through their calm presence, empaths have pretty an impact in phrases of alleviating the struggling of others. As an empath who has learned to constant themselves, your mere presence may be a recuperation balm to others. You tremendous want to show up, and each person else feels cushty. You probably understand one or of such human beings on your life. Their presence makes you experience steady and comfortable as despite the fact that the entirety within the universe is aligned as it ought to be. If you do now not comprehend everybody like that, it honestly might be which you are that man or woman. You may unknowingly be the calming presence in human beings's lives. What a tremendous superpower to have, with a purpose to meet with a chum for coffee, simply understand the trouble they may be experiencing, and provide them beneficial solutions. Of direction, the essential detail to remember with this superpower is which you have to heal your self first. You can not repair one of a kind people's wounds at the same time as yours are bleeding.

The Superpower of Creativity

Empaths are relatively gifted and innovative. It most effective makes revel in—you can't be so particularly talented and fail to make a few issue out of it. Many empaths skip immediately to create track that lasts generations, make art work that wows the entire global for years, or write novels that captivate thousands and lots of human beings. It is uncommon to find out an empath who does now not have a modern bone of their frame. Creativity is the empath's outlet. Creativity is the empath's chance to pour their souls out with out being judged for it. Think approximately it: the empath who has needed to warfare their feelings, in any other case referred to as demons, all their lifestyles regularly dreams a secure place wherein he or she will be capable of explicit precisely what they enjoy. This empath will flip to a platform along with painting, creating a music, workout, drawing, movie-making, writing and each one of a kind innovative outlet that lets in for freedom of expression. It isn't any wonder that masses of creatives give you ideas that have all of us else thinking why nobody idea of that earlier than. It is in fact due to the fact the thoughts of an empath is like a by no means-finishing maze with surprises at every corner. The nicely of creativity that an empath embodies can in no manner run dry. And the first rate element is that the empath feels their art. The artwork comes from deep down inner them, and on the same time mirrors the feelings of the people round them due to the truth the empath is able to be selfless of their paintings.

Using Your Superpowers to Impact the World

When used efficiently, the superpowers of an empath have the capacity to trade lives. Whether at artwork or in personal relationships, an empath's intuitive functionality is their first-rate asset. As an empath, you've got were given something that many human beings war to have: the capability to examine a state of affairs proper away and not using a want to invite questions. Coupled with the superpowers mentioned before, it's clean to appearance that empaths have a whole lot of capacity to effect people and organizations everywhere they bypass. The apparent question, therefore, will become, how does an empath skip approximately the technique of channeling their superpowers towards the right reasons? In wonderful phrases, how can you take benefit of what you have to decorate your life and people of others?

Creative Direction

Because in their fairly intuitive nature, empaths regularly are available to be had with regards to imparting modern path in art work initiatives or maybe in their own lives. Creativity is in no way typically the direct cease stop end result of natural accurate judgment. For artwork to enchantment to its target audience, there needs to be an detail of intuitiveness and heartfelt emotion. That is why some of the maximum celebrated authors of all time are generally individuals who write with severa unhappiness. They are capable of draw emotions from their readers due to the fact they feel and recognize those emotions.

Ernest Hemingway, a worldwide-famous American journalist and author, as quickly as positioned it aptly this way: "There's not something to writing. All you do is sit down down at a typewriter and bleed." In this declaration, Hemingway modified into recognizing the thankless tough paintings that is writing and on the same time appreciating that the magic of paintings can not exist without feeling or emotion.

As an empath operating inside the current industry, you need to in no way shy away from sharing your opinions and perspectives on projects. Some of them would possibly probable seem outlandish or ridiculous but it's miles regularly the ambitious empath who's willing to position on their innovative heart on their sleeve that wins the day and inspires others.

Nurturing Relationships

Psychic empaths make extremely good buddies. They are high-quality listeners. They are empathetic. They count on extremely good human beings's desires. They are often nurturing and infrequently judgmental. One psychic empath friend is definitely well worth ten inside the bush, so to talk. When a psychic empath meets a nicely-that means character with whom they will be capable of nurture a deferential and together useful courting, their friendship blossoms for years and years. It is sincerely a factor to be pleased with if you are an empath because of the truth you'll be this kind of high-quality buddy to the individuals who need you.

Empaths aren't simply nurturing to their friends. They increase this trait to their colleagues as properly. Work environments can frequently be ridden with tension and other types of toxicity. For someone who isn't attuned to or who isn't capable of understand this horrible strength, such art work environments may be very distressing. Empaths can filter out thru precise kinds of energy and reap critical insights which allow them to navigate any environment mindfully. As such, empaths are possibly to make thoughtful colleagues who anticipate earlier than they bounce and who try to recognize in which others are coming earlier than judging harshly.

Besides friendships and paintings relationships, empaths additionally thrive as parents. Empath dad and mom often have masses notable energy, encouragement, and empowerment to pour into their children. After all, an empath knows what ails their little one despite the fact that the kid isn't in a role to articulate it. As an empath, whether or not you choose to have natural kids or adopt kids who want a domestic, there is a robust chance that you'll be this form of mother and father who grow as lots as end up satisfactory pals with their kids.

Mediation Roles

Because they are capable of recognize humans with out requiring phrases to be stated, empaths often make superb mediators in conflict decision. Their capability to find out problems earlier than they escalate into larger troubles permits the empath to be one step beforehand in times of battle. At the same time, they're also able to dig deep into a person's psyche and recognize their great wants and needs, and thus realign the mediation workout to do the equal thing, which guarantees that all parties experience like they've been listened to.

Activists and Advocates

As an empath, you've got the functionality to endorse for the unseen and the unheard because of the truth you're able to see and pay interest them. An empath's deep connection with their surrounding permits them to have a heightened information of issues. While some humans will muddle and shrug it off, an empath will find out it particularly disconcerting to move about life with such an obvious disregard for others and mainly for the surroundings. It is, therefore, now common to locate many empaths regarding themselves in advocacy roles which embody preventing in competition to environmental pollutants, being activists for human and animal rights, or even supporting to bring the marginalized to the leading edge. In the eyes of the empath, social injustices can not and want to never be overlooked.

What's even better is that empaths are capable of join with out issues with human beings, and for this reason influencing humans to join worthy reasons comes absolutely to them. When an empath pleads their case, it's almost not possible to dismiss.

Career Choices

The outstanding careers for empaths are folks that allow them to live out their whole capability as healers and caregivers with out burdening them unfairly with emotional and mental drain. If an empath makes a choice to move down a extra draining route, but notwithstanding the fact that feels fulfilled in doing what they do, it's important for them to discover ways to deal with themselves so they'll be no longer wiped out on a everyday basis. In careers where an empath is constantly uncovered to the suffering of others or immoderate degrees of drama and negativity, it's quite vital that the empath develops wholesome coping and protective mechanisms to keep away from emotional drain.

There are positive careers which can be better right for empaths for severa motives. Empaths, as an example, make extraordinary artists. As referred to in advance, they'll be capable of feel deeply and this gives them a innovative part over everyone else. A clever individual as soon as stated that life imitates art work. By deciding on to grow to be an artist, an empath is basically lighting fixtures a torch to show the relaxation of the arena the way to stay. A remarkable advantage of being an artist is which you don't even need to reveal your face to the relaxation of the sector. You can permit your paintings to talk on your behalf whilst defensive your self from public interest, that could frequently be overwhelming. An artist who has selected this method is Banksy. Banksy, now 45-years antique and based totally completely in England, has controlled to steer the arena along together with his paintings while preserving his anonymity. His debut as a road artist became decrease once more within the 1990s and up to now, nobody has been able to unveil his real identification.

Freelance writing and journey blogging are other profession choices which may be exceptional for the empath who wants to discover their innovative thing, impact human beings, float freely, and recharge their minds and our bodies while preserving human interplay to a minimal. To be clean, this isn't to mention that empaths hate going for walks with humans. Rather, empaths thrive more and make higher use in their superpowers once they paintings in environments that allow their inclined aspects to flourish with out horrific strength.

As an empath, you could moreover maintain in thoughts becoming a web teach or therapist. In each cases, you may be supporting others and due to the fact there are tips to the form of care you want to provide, you're able to help others whilst moreover safeguarding yourself. Other examples of consistent and captivating career routes for empaths encompass charity, social work, and healthcare, particularly highbrow healthcare. Empaths moreover make incredible veterinarians for the cause that they're capable of deeply deal with animals.

Overall, empaths do properly in self-employment and in professions in which they will be able to assist others. When an empath is in a profession that may be a fine in form for his or her character, they leave a super effect that resonates with each person they come into touch with.

As an empath, you could have formerly struggled with keeping down a hobby. It is important to understand that this can be due to the fact you had decided on the wrong form of method, or intuitively, your soul have come to be trying to tell you that there is some issue else accessible a lot higher suitable you. Something your soul is yearning to express. With the right profession, you can exchange lives.

Another path to recollect as an empath is an entrepreneurship. This also can moreover sound daunting at the start however permit's break it down on why that is a awesome concept. Being an entrepreneur offers a terrific enjoy of freedom, which all empaths love. You set your very very own regulations and your personal artwork time table. You aren't high-quality through the regulations of having a boss. You do now not need to ask for permission while to take a holiday or while to go to the rest room. Additionally, within the region of entrepreneurship, you need to apprehend what the market goals. You should be capable of provide to the market with a few issue they may be glad with. Something that is going to solve their hassle. This is wherein the empath is surely able to shine. Using their final present of empathy, they are capable of in fact dive into the mind of the marketplace and in fact recognize their pains and problems. And with this, can supply a product to the market that satisfies drastically. Entrepreneurship additionally acts as a medium wherein the empath can unharness their creativity and offer you with thoughts and answers, bringing superb satisfaction to the empath.

The worst careers for empaths consist of the ones which require one to be aggressive and aggressive, deal with crowds, engage with quite a few people, and play through policies which may be on occasion unreasonable or perhaps unscrupulous. Professions the sort of politics, sales, and public own family members don't healthful most empaths.

Detecting Manipulation

An empath's potential to experience a person's terrible power even if the person is trying to cover it as some thing else permits them to tell while someone is lying, despite the fact that each person else may be within the dark. An empath who has discovered to recognize particular people's energies without getting drawn into them is capable of enjoy diffused electricity shifts which may additionally moreover moreover factor in the direction of functionality manipulation. Manipulators use the identical e-book of guidelines along with the use of frame language and eye contact to create rapport with the cause of creating an aura of harmlessness. For the green eye, this type of rapport can also come across as actual. Fortunately for empaths, inauthenticity is often detected from a mile away.

This capability allows empaths to guard themselves and people round them from predators who can be seeking to take benefit. Since time immemorial, kids were implored to pay attention to their moms thinking about the fact that "mothers comprehend awesome." The reason for this is that mothers are pretty intuitive in the course of their children and are consequently capable of expect chance even in advance than the youngsters can experience it. That is why your well-that means mother would possibly take one take a look at a woman pal or boyfriend that you have in reality delivered to her and can help you realize which you're about to get into hassle. This shape of 6th sense that mothers have closer to their offspring is the equal that empaths have within the course of maximum humans and situations.

Diffusing Negative Energy

The energy of an empath is light and exceptional via the use of nature. When they're overwhelmed with the useful resource of different people's horrible energies, empaths have a tendency to be the slight in the darkness. Just with the aid of being found in a place, an empath could make human beings experience lightness and positivity that starkly contrasts the power that is regularly emitted through predators.

Even if you're shy to talk to human beings and hate crowded settings, you may use your mere presence to make others enjoy higher. Sometimes, terms aren't even required. There is a lot terrible electricity in the worldwide that it makes all the distinction if one character can be that lighthouse inside the dark that indicates the ones stranded in the darkish sea that there's desire in the horizon.

Chapter 7: Best Techniques To Block Or Overlook Approximately A Person's Negativity

Whilst simplified techniques are splendid for moderate kinds of psychic attack – recollect, they're now not all planned, or immoderate – there are instances while you will be coping with a quite relentless, and prolonged assault for your emotions, with the beneficial aid of human beings inside your close to circle.

At such times, you can need to exercising a more forceful shape of self-defence. They do no longer need to be risky to the opportunity character, although it is possible to deliver any intentionally terrible moves over again. For example, use the Wiccan Law of Threefold-Return, and the depth felt with the useful resource of them will triple, but as formerly stated; the wrongdoer may not take heed to their movements, and do you actually need to harm a person who's unknowing?

The following meditation is one I frequently use; in particular once I enjoy my strength stages are waning, regardless of the cause at the back of the depletion. It's in particular useful after an 'assault' episode, and may be finished any time of day, and is a manner that could dispense recuperation, further to electricity.

It's pretty an concerned machine for a beginner to attempt consequently I recommend you report the method both onto your iPod, MP3 player or cell cellular telephone. You'll need to talk slowly and in a properly-modulated tone.

Sit or lie, in a stable quiet location and close to your eyes and calm your respiratory.

Picture for your mind's eye, a large bubble of iridescent golden strength. This bubble is sizeable. Taller than you are, and wider than you are.

Imagine your self stepping near the bubble, and as you do, you'll be conscious that it seems to have a life all of its non-public. Its electricity will shimmer and ripple, and as you pay attention there'll be a moderate fizzing noise similar to the static from a radio.

Visualise yourself stepping even nearer, till you're stood immediately within the front of the bubble. Do not be worried, as there's no risk worried, and the power contained inner is 'recuperation' electricity.

Stretch your palms out inside the the front of you, and watch them slip resultseasily via the strength wall. You'll enjoy a moderate tingle in competition to your pores and skin however no extra than that.

Gradually, as rapid, or slowly as you want, step into the bubble, till you're completely surrounded through the golden energy. It may be above you, underneath you, and all around you. Wherever you appearance all you'll see is a beautiful yellow-gold, fizzing power.

Unexpectedly you'll feel your better frame begin to tilt backwards. Your ft will raise from the ground, and also you'll discover yourself lying willing, floating on an energy cloud in the bubble. You'll be suspended in region, however certainly robust. The energy under your outstretched body will make sure you enjoy such as you're lying on a slight bed

As you're lying there, truly comfortable, eyes closed, recall this splendid strength entering all of the spectrums of your air of secrecy, searching out injuries, leakages, or foreign power-signatures that could need recovery assist......There'll no longer be a centimetre of your aura un-tormented by this tremendously essential stress.

Should you choice, you could ask your manual(s), or angel(s) to face with you and watch over you at the same time as rejuvenation takes vicinity? It might also take numerous minutes.....Do now not rush the gadget.

Once finished, thank any divine presence which you trust is with you, and deliver them on their manner. When organized, open your eyes. You'll enjoy alert, and the golden energy will maintain to do its paintings as you keep on together along with your day.

Requesting your Spirit Guide's Assistance

As earlier than; find out a tranquil strong vicinity to sit or lie. Close your eyes and calm your respiration.

Once you're cushty, I need you to call your maximum spirit manual, preferably with the resource of their call, if you realize it. Alternatively, ask for one in all your protective spirits to appear in advance than you to your thoughts's eye – If you desire, you may request that your parent angel seem. Yes! They are separate entities – it can take a few moments, but in a few instances, they will had been looking to your call, and could seem right away.

If you do now not visualise a face, or a spirit, do not be involved. They may select to appear as a coloration, or a particular image. Rather than seen proof, you need to search for sentient proof. For example: has the surroundings modified? Become gentler, or quieter? Is there a certain perfume, that wasn't there in advance than? Do you just 'revel in' you're not by myself? Spirit art work in mysterious strategies.

Once you agree with there's every different presence (they're now not volatile, simplest useful) greet them correctly. Explain which you believe; you're being psychically attacked with the aid of each extraordinary man or woman. Request they approach the offender's maximum spirit guide at the way to asking their fee (the sender) to desist, because it will handiest purpose them karmic damage in the long-run.

Once you've got exceeded this mission to your manual, bear in mind they'll act upon it as quick as viable.....Thank them for acting, and wave them off.

Finally, placed your shielding bubble in place earlier than taking off your eyes

It is feasible to finish a meditation, whereby you request the Vampire give up their actions, but, for my part I believe a stronger have an effect on is required, and as fast as each facets' spirit courses are added into the equation, there may be more chance of a brief selection.

Three Most Common Ways to Expend or Use Energy:

Trying to assist or "restore" special human beings, or their issues.

Burning highbrow strength even as searching for to address someone, or a scenario.

Going in opposition to the natural go along with the float of the universe, or searching out to force a excellent final results.

These 3 topics are onerous. Our non secular our our our bodies can, and often will, expend an entire lot of power on a daily foundation relying on how we pick out to apply it.

More importantly, this may moreover be determined via who we surround ourselves with. Other people can and could drain power from your tool within the try and recharge their very very own device.

Part of the cause electricity vampires experience so well after they're spherical those folks that they're drawn to is due to the fact they may be essentially being recharged via the alternative individual; in different terms, they're stealing power faraway from them. If you are that precise person, however, it leaves you feeling tired and seeking to take a nap, due to the fact masses of your electricity has just been excessive jacked!

Energy vampires aren't constantly strangers; in reality, typically they're near pals and circle of relatives people. Unfortunately 70% of the population has a bent to offer and keep a lower vibration.

So if you're one of the 30% who tend to maintain a higher vibration more often than now not, you're most likely surrounded with the useful resource of power vampires in essential terms through information. It can be in reality, clearly difficult whilst you're one of the 30% and also you're spherical a person who holds a low vibration.

It clearly may want to make you experience bodily uncomfortable.

Why?

Because at the same time as your vibration is low you don't reproduce the identical amount energetically as while your vibration is immoderate. When your vibration is immoderate, you constantly fill up yourself, while your vibration is low, this doesn't appear; you've got were given what is known as an energy leakage. In distinct phrases, you received't maintain a charge for extremely lengthy.

If you may't hold a price, you'll be in everyday need of replenishment.

People who keep a low vibration will drain their battery three to 4 times faster than folks that keep a higher vibration.

When you maintain a better vibration, you could basically become a goal for power vampires with out even understanding it. How do you grow to be a aim?

Happy human beings provide a excessive vibration, and at the same time as glad humans are spherical individuals who aren't so glad (low vibration), you have got mismatched vibrations, and each vibrations turns into magnified.

Your vibration (whether or not or now not or not it is high or low) becomes very widespread, internally. It doesn't matter quantity in case you're the unhappy or unhappy one, it'll have this shape of effect. If your vibration is higher than the opportunity person, it becomes very major to you. If your vibration is lower than the other character, it'll also come to be very apparent. When you're the sad one, generally your first response is to make this magnified unhappy feeling, or low vibration (which has now become undeniably the focus of your interest), to save you. You without a doubt want this feel to head away, you don't need to be so aware about it. It doesn't experience accurate! The quickest manner to make this sense depart is to supply the other character's vibration right all the way down to your degree. Bring it down so that you're a better vibrational in shape. The nearer your vibration is to some other individual, the an awful lot less you phrase the mismatched vibrations, and the higher you feel, so problem solved!

They will say horrible subjects to you; some issue that makes you enjoy horrible, so your vibration is reduced.

Chapter 8: Strategies To Cope With Energy Vampires At Paintings

I need to touch on one problem one more time, it's the difficulty of having rid of an electricity vampire from your life. This have to doubtlessly be pretty a tough factor to do, particularly if you have an entire lot of emotional ties with the person concerned. Fortunately no matter the reality that, it could be finished, however it is able to take a bit of labor to your element.

Is it your boss?

If your boss is continuously getting you down no matter how properly you do at paintings, you can want to maintain in thoughts walking somewhere else. If you don't want to get a brand new method, otherwise you absolutely cannot discover work a few location else, don't fear, you obtained't continuously sense which encompass you're caught in a rut.

Remember that grumpy and nasty bosses often have wounded personalities. For a few purpose, being in fee of diverse humans and making them feel lousy, makes them revel in higher.

Use the techniques defined on this ebook to protect yourself from those bad energies that frequently drain you.

Is it your accomplice?

Sometimes everybody have to mention 'Goodbye' to a person and bypass on. If leaving your power-draining partner isn't always an alternative, there can be distinctive strategies to deal with the manner they make you sense.

Why no longer strive talking to them about how they make you feel? This can take quite a few bravery, however within the occasion that they definitely care about you, they will pay interest. If this isn't always an opportunity then please keep in mind the usage of the techniques defined on this e-book.

Is it your buddy?

If your pal is continuously draining your excessive nice energy, perhaps it's now time to allow them to move. Perhaps you can need to take into account seeing them masses less often, so they're now not a large part of your lifestyles any greater.

You and your pal can also have had a few perfect times collectively. You might also moreover have even grown up together, and taking walks away can also seem difficult. Remember, you don't need to stroll away without a doubt, however seeing them an entire lot lots much less often will assist to make sure your energy is not worn-out as a bargain.

Who is aware of, by the time you spot them all over again, you can have armed yourself with the competencies you want to preserve that bad energy away.

Remember that simplest you may determine the manner you react to a high quality situation. With the assist of the techniques I've described, you should be capable of make a large alternate in your electricity.

So I'm going to provide you 3 recommendations on a manner to take away awful energy at paintings

Number one:

You cannot manipulate what others count on or say about you. You can't please genuinely anybody. And in case you are a person who lives continuously thinking about what others are pronouncing or thinking about you, opportunities are you're continuously carrying the electricity of those human beings.

When you reflect onconsideration on someone who has completed some aspect terrible to you, who has said a few issue negative approximately you, you are constantly feeding the ones human beings together with your personal electricity! Even worse: you're sporting the energy of these human beings in your decrease lower back!

So, the brilliant that you can do is to offer them a fantastic deal less importance. Of route, it's simpler stated than accomplished, however here's a terrific method: each time a horrible idea pops into your mind, try to recollect a few factor else; consider a song, a person you want, recollect a place you enjoy, your favored food, or any other element that allows you exchange the image this is now crossing your thoughts.

Number

It's very important that you discover ways to make a distinction between individuals who need help, who need your aid or love, from folks that handiest need to suck your energy out; the energy vampires.

There's not anything incorrect with saying "no" each time it's essential to say "no"!

And quantity 3

Spend greater time in nature! Spend more time in contact with wood, with plant life, with grass, via the sea...

Walk barefoot at the land, at the seashore sand, and opt for walks in places wherein trees are plentiful.

Crystals are critical elements of nature, near doing away with bad energies. In the areas you spend maximum of it sluggish, have a few crystals; in your artwork region, for instance, and commonly deliver a crystal with you.

Chapter 9: Easy And Effective Strategies To Block Energy Vampires

By now, it has turn out to be clear that empaths need to do high-quality matters to manipulate and address being empaths. The following coping practices can assist empaths to make the most of their talents and gain manage over them:

1. Shielding: Create a protect among you and the severa feelings and feelings coming from others. This is commonly completed via visualizing a effective wall of natural electricity reputation among you and precise people's feelings, set this wall of herbal power to selective, allowing you to handiest word others emotions best in case you need to.

2. Set limits and obstacles: Know which you can not continuously be a hero for others. Often, let them undergo by myself their burdens. Their troubles must by no means turn out to be your non-public due

to the reality you have your very very very own troubles too. Do not allow yourself to emerge as a dumping ground. If you do no longer set limits and boundaries, you could hold dropping your self and feeling feelings that are not your own to the detriment of yourself in the end.

You want to moreover spend lots less time with places, subjects and those that drain your strength. Stay far from emotional vampires.

three. Avoid duties that are not yours: As an empath, you may be feeling such as you normally meant to take care of others and be there for them but it isn't right to constantly feel in my opinion liable for others. Learn not to transport beyond your capability, studies that you cannot usually be the hero.

four. Cleanse your self frequently: From time to time, metaphysically sweep out all of the emotions and emotions that aren't yours or pressure will boom and weigh down you. This is a intellectual exercising that can be achieved through a few aspect like meditation.

5. Beware of horrific energies: Never allow yourself to continuously share the sufferings and tragedies of the arena. Unless you can perform a touch trouble to save you them, for example, do now not constantly positioned your self to experience what the patients of cruelty feel. This does not suggest you have to reduce rate or forget approximately terrible facts or struggling that isn't always yours but really sharing in dreadful events now not frequently serves any nicely cause.

6. Embrace your presents: You did not choose out to be an empath, however you're one. You may also moreover moreover like or dislike that fact however

one aspect you have to recognize is that the great component to do is to encompass being an empath and constantly work on your self just so with every new day, being an empath will become a blessing and now not a curse.

7. Ask for assist: It is good enough to inform others approximately your private problems or how being an empath feels. Look for assist, all of us need each other so you also can rely on human beings you accept as actual with that will help you address any trouble you is probably handling whether or no longer or no longer it's far due to being an empath or no longer. Feel unfastened to lean on others.

Chapter 10: How To Guard Myself From Unwanted Psychic Readings, What Is The Great Crystal For Recuperation Negativity?

Cleanse Your Aura from Negative and Self-Destructive Thoughts

Our intellectual self is continuously speaking with super human beings's mental self, therefore allowing us to soak up horrible mind, feelings, and emotions from others. We create our very very own thoughts, feelings, and emotions, plenty of which are not constant with our first rate hobbies. As an empath, you need to growth your awareness of different varieties of thoughts in conjunction with terrible, repetitive, redundant, and automated mind. One of the remarkable procedures to realize approximately your idea sample is to keep a track of your mind with a notebook.

Acknowledge each concept that you've skilled over a 24 hour duration. You'll be taken aback to apprehend how hard it is able to be to preserve a song of your emotions, emotions, and thoughts. When we've got first-rate mind, they align with our revel in-nicely vibrations, for this reason major to greater balance, peace, restoration, and harmony. When those thoughts are bad, they bring about about limitations and blockages.

Negative mind are fed to us over many years, mainly at the same time as they are related to a enormously annoying experience. These poor thoughts are everyday through awful tales, expectancies, and times. The more they'll be fed the extra active and powerful they end up. Their impact for your united states of america of thoughts and highbrow balance grows stronger. These terrible mind and feelings can be based totally on particular human beings's reviews and expectations. They are capable of gambling out several instances for your mind at the same time as going undetected till you prevent feeding the monster. Pay attention for your perception styles closely.

Thoughts which are a stop end result of fear, insecurity, grief, anger, and blame live interior your power vicinity for prolonged to purpose extra vibration in alignment with those energies. Over a time body, the ones motive someone to draw comparable existence research. These concept forms might also then vibrate indoors us in a way in which they catalyze reactions in any respect energy frame ranges, which includes physical, intellectual and spiritual.

The mind motive us attracting humans, critiques, and times that align with them. It is similar to attracting low energies that preserve on your strength. To break free from the sample, perceive your life extra objectively to gauge if you are drawing unwanted situations. If you're continually attracting things you do no longer desire, you could well be vibrating in line with these objects with out aware recognition. Ensure you check in in conjunction with your electricity area multiple instances to decide in case you frequently revel in worn-out, burdened and depressed to selecting up or developing terrible belief office work, and permit them to transport.

Repeat Mantras

One of the proper and only techniques to cleanse your energy is to exercise deep respiratory and mantra recitation for preventing awful power. When negativity hits, right now reputation on the breathing for a while. Breathe deeply and exhale the discomfort causing electricity. Gradually, breathing eliminates negativity from the frame. Repeat a effective mantra of your preference three times in a voice and tone that establishes that you honestly imply what you are reciting. You can say some issue together with, "cross lower back this energy to its sender with compassion." The command of your voice can pressure out pain from the body. Your respiration turns into the technique thru which the electricity is released once more into the universe's power region.

While reciting this effective mantra, the empath can breathe out their poisonous strength from the lumbar spine into the decrease lower back. The gap a number of the lumbar vertebras permits the elimination of bad energy from the frame. Imagine the pain exiting through those channels within the spine. Say "I release the power" more than one times as it's miles released from the body, and blends with the larger than lifestyles matrix.

Seek out Like-Minded Empaths

This might not be a cleaning recurring regular with se. However, it's going to can help you attain out to different empaths and observe their unique survival competencies. As steady with studies, really 1 out of 5 humans are real empaths. Since they aren't present within the majority, it is crucial to search for your very personal kinds. Even inside empaths, there are unique sorts of empaths at the side of nature empaths, earth empaths and so on.

Look out for empaths on on line assembly websites and boards by searching with the assist of key phrases like empathy, spirituality, empath, and one-of-a-kind related phrases. Hanging out with empaths on your neighborhood or locality is likewise a superb idea. Just make certain which you aren't soaking up their 2nd-hand energy to experience even greater miserable. The idea is to connect with each fantastic to construct a resource employer that offers greater positivity, notion, and encouragement and does now not go away you even more worn-out. Websites such as Meetup.Com will let you locate fellow empaths to loaf around with. Learn about individuals who've had memories just like yours on social media, and connect with them at a deeper diploma to undertake their coping strategies.

Online media stimulates your feelings and emotions. It can purpose everything from a experience of happiness to sleeplessness to helplessness. Empaths are hypersensitive to energies floating within the physical further to virtual plane. This method you need to make sure you don't spend vain time seeking out to engage in sports activities activities that do not restore positivity, empathy, and sensitivity in you.

Nurture yourself via using conducting a healthy balance of on line and offline activities which includes meditation, yoga, lengthy walks in nature and so on that nourish and repair your spirit. Empaths can be their private exceptional friends in severa techniques.

Practice a Space and Water Cleansing Ritual

Empaths can increase an internal and outside cleaning ritual that permits them maintain equilibrium internal an critical power middle- the sacral chakra. It can every be executed through a easy approach with the aid of using the usage of consuming a glass of water and imagining being cleansed interior out, taking a shower, playing a dip inside the lake, a herbal heat spring tub and so on. A lot of empaths purify or cleanse their strength by means of manner of visualizing exquisite body additives being wiped clean every outside and inside. Imagine a ray of white light clearing all of your unwanted electricity as you pour water over your frame. This effective white mild ray is cleansing your body, mind, and spirit internally and externally.

Empaths also can use techniques together with Reiki to purify power spherical their physical area. There are multiple Reiki techniques that assist you to cleanse the strength or purify spaces around you to depart you feeling more nurtured, powerful, and energized. Place tiny saltwater bowls (a cup of water blended with 2-three tablespoons of sea salt works first-rate) inside the corners of your room, domestic, place of business or any area you want to purify. Let the bowls continue to be in the given vicinity in a single day in order that they soak up all of the antique, unwanted, and negative strength from the distance. Discard the ones bowls day after today. This is a excellent every day practice for empaths to smooth their bodily region off from undesirable strength.

Your domestic is a sacred area, where you come back to escape all horrible energies that hold straight away to you. One sturdy tip for defensive the purity of the gap or protective yourself from unfavourable emotions is to form a crystal grid round the gap. Black tourmaline is an increasingly defensive crystal. Keep a black tourmaline piece at the doorway of residence, room, or place of work to keep terrible energies at bay. If you are already feeling beaten through the awful electricity, location a tourmaline piece in every corner of your room with tiny sea salt water bowls to absorb the negativity.

Practicing sage purification with the cause of keeping off unwelcome energy that has accompanied you domestic maintains your location and spiritual psyche free from being clouded through the day's awful and destructive energy. As the empath sages, the purifying smoke need to be allowed to drift into areas of the room, which can be a magnet for maximum traffic. Pay cautious interest and do no longer avoid regions which encompass closets, doors, and domestic domestic home windows.

Once this emotional palette cleansing approach is mastered, start placing healthy boundaries inner your air of mystery. Take these steps for retaining and protecting your power as an empath, on the manner to will will let you view the sector with a more inspiring and top notch mind-set via stabilizing your mindset and mood. As an empath, you may carefully discover ways to understand this is your energy, and which power is in truth being dumped on you from outside undesirable property. You will discover ways to decide precisely at the same time as the have an impact on of your strength ends and the strength of various people begins offevolved.

Another famous purification technique is giving your self Reiki each day to cleanse all of the built-up power. Start through giving yourself Reiki for 5 minutes every day. Gradually boom it to 7 mins, and sooner or later make it 10 minutes consistent with day. This easy but powerful workout will assist defend and hold you energetically.

Each time one taps into Reiki, that is the universe's purest strength form, there may be an automated alignment that paperwork a safety envelope over you. There were innumerable instances in which Reiki practitioners have been able to effectively detach from particular people's horrible energies. You can learn how to provide your self Reiki with the useful resource of enlisting the assist of Reiki grasp near you.

It may also moreover take you several days to paintings together with your electricity and understand the strength of using your sensitivity or empath objects to help terrific human beings or remodel their lives whilst though keeping your energy. One of the most vital topics to maintain in my mind in your adventure as an empath is, which will grow to be a beacon of notion and transformation and lead others, you have to look after your nicely-being and strength protection.

You can stay inside your active strength best while you're capable of annoying for, nurturing, and retaining your personal electricity. Learn to cleanse and purify your self internal your very private active electricity in choice to centering yourself on awesome people's terrible energies.

Another method that works wonderfully properly for a few empaths in terms of purifying their strength or place is the introduction of easy vegetation. These are flowers you experience attracted or interested in at an inner stage. They provide an proper away enhance of energy and feelings that assist you repair, nurture, rejuvenate, and reboot your body, mind, and soul. The upkeep and nurturing stand up at a deeper diploma at the same time as elements of nature are concerned due to the reality at some diploma we are all related with the universe. When we align with nature, there may be a more feel of positivity and oneness with nature. Fresh flora also can be pretty recovery and healing.

Visualization and Crystal Meditation

This is some different fantastic power cleansing approach for empaths. Start via manner of manner of being seated in a distraction-unfastened, calm, and comfortable vicinity. Close your eyes. Visualize shielding or protecting your self from undesirable and awful electricity. This permits in developing the crucial energy limitations amongst your and special humans's energies. There are a couple of visualization strategies for empaths. Use the number one one within the morning proper away after waking, and earlier than going to bed at night. Standstill, and take deep breaths, on the same time as outstretching your arms. Visualize your self with a big knife reducing via the bodily frame, as in developing a lessen from your form. Visualize the knife removing your active ties, awful energy, and undesirable attachments. This helps you to align with freeing the electricity of unwanted feelings that preserve you once more. While working towards this visualization, empaths can also hold a chunk of black tourmaline in every hand.

In many instances, empaths visualize a circle of mild encircling them, in which absolutely everyone's thoughts, emotions, and emotions live. While interacting with distinctive people, we make it a point to draw from the entirety that is true for us in location of the way the alternative character is feeling or what they want to be aware of in the meanwhile. Think approximately conditions at the same time as you are having a particularly emotionally charged verbal exchange with someone. As empaths, we regularly revel in like changing our phrases, technique of delivery and actions primarily based totally on how the opposite individual is responding or feeling. In first rate times, this allows us to confuse our maximum honest efforts to assertively country some issue the other individual desires to understand. For example, we can also positioned an prevent to a romantic relationship, but we also can face hassle affirming it because we anticipate the opportunity individual may not take it too nicely. Imagine a circle that we could us grow to be compassionate and emotionally aware on the identical time as being grounded emotionally from wherein we originate at the same time as articulating our emotions, emotions, choices, and options.

The next visualization exercising consists of making prepared your self mentally in advance than experiencing a worrying situation. For instance, as an empath who may work in the midst of some of people, moving into the proper mind-set is crucial before stepping into a place in which you're likely to come across some of human beings. To exercising this, take a seat down despite the fact that for your car or every other serene place in advance than certainly taking walks inside the course of a whole lot of humans. Take deep, prolonged breaths. Once you've identified your center, consider a huge bubble round you. This bubble is the protect that protects you from specific humans's strength promote off.

Use a high-quality mantra or confirmation consisting of, "I sense protected, nurtured, preserved and shielded." Feel that the protect is powerful enough to get rid of any capability toxic electricity this is possibly to make its way to you. Once you're assured of this feeling, end the visualization, and mantra chanting. Put a selenite necklace around the neck. This can be one of the best practices to dam your self from energies that don't belong to you. Selenite helps empaths take away power that isn't theirs and lets in keep a enjoy of stability and harmony. It is likewise beneficial in terms of shielding and clearing their electricity vicinity to make certain that the energy that is part of it's far their personal and doesn't belong to everyone else.

Another powerful power cleansing and shield ritual for empaths is crystal meditation. Meditating with crystals help increase an empath's emotional and intellectual properly-being, while letting them cut ties with power vampires who are forever sapping their energy. Black kyanite is pretty powerful for empaths as it will become their sword for snapping unwanted and adverse ties. As an empath, your electricity place is blanketed from folks who prey on your positivity and unload their negativity on you.

When your private energy feels sapped and worn-out, align with kyanite's energy. This compels you to observe what's bringing you down, and the way you can avoid it. You will examine to distinguish between your and unique people's energy, for that reason freeing strength that does not belong to you or strength you are forcefully stuck with. This will initiate the approach of freeing pent-up poisonous negativity. These crystals work with all electricity chakras to get your energy venture into alignment. Keep black kyanite inside the hand, at the identical time as utilizing all over your frame speedy as you visualize decreasing ties with undesirable and negative energies originating from others.

Follow Your Dreams

As an empath, you could get majorly stuck in special human beings's dramas to care about your non-public dreams, dreams, and possibilities. Give hobby to motive in life. What do you want to carry out? What do you aspire to be? What is your purpose in existence? Remove the time to take a seat down and workout your goals, goals, dreams, and dreams. Chalk out a plant to perform them in location of focusing your energy on unique people and their drama. To accomplish your life motive, you can have to learn how to be greater assertive and refuse distinct humans, even as subjects do no longer align together with your general life cause.

Find the right balance among being there for other humans and making time for yourself. Standing up for yourself doesn't make you a horrific or selfish man or woman. It way you care about supporting yourself and looking after your properly-being as hundreds as you care about others. Being an empath isn't just a present but moreover a large duty, which furthermore manner you have a responsibility toward your self, to look out to your very very very own well-being, happiness, and welfare. Try to be beneficial in preference to helping every pained human you stumble upon, who drains your recognition, strength, and priorities.

By following a group of these survival and cleansing tips, an empath can lead a extra emotionally balanced and advanced lifestyles that permits them encourage, encourage and uplift one of a kind people through living our dreams and lifestyles reason. This is extra important than seeking to constantly guide others on the price of your very own nicely-being, sanity, and life desires.

Chapter 11: What Can I Do If I Am The Hassle An Active Vampire?

Are you an electricity vampire?

At a few degree in our lives we have were given all been an strength vampire. We have all had instances at the same time as we've performed the victim and desired a bit of interest, or we've even been aggressive to others. But have you ever ever ever considered that you can nonetheless be an energy vampire?

The trouble is that it can be so easy for every human beings to become a vampire with out noticing. Think of the very last time you felt a bit down, did your mere presence deliver different human beings down too?

One morning I awakened feeling irritable because of a dream I had. I began out my day entire of poor energy and I unknowingly transferred this onto my companion because as soon as I spoke I sounded and behaved irritably.

This have become obviously not a fantastic start to the day, and as we ate breakfast collectively, I moaned at her and unconsciously tired her energy. My partner occurred to be suffering from some troubles herself on the time, so my moaning sincerely didn't help in any respect. After breakfast we each went off to paintings feeling lots less than glad, and we no doubt unfold that irritability to others thru-out the day.

It's very easy to rub your feelings off onto other humans. Think of these instances you've met up with a chum and gossiped negatively approximately a person. You every move home with more terrible mind

approximately the person who might not
have finished something incorrect within
the first area.